The Ruin of Representation in Modernist Art and Texts

Studies in the Fine Arts:
Art Theory, No. 13

Donald B. Kuspit, Series Editor

Professor of Art History
State University of New York at Stony Brook

Other Titles in This Series

The Ruin of Representation in Modernist Art and Texts

by
Jo Anna Isaak

U·M·I Research Press

Ann Arbor, Michigan

Chapter 2 was first published in *MOSAIC: A Journal for the Interdisciplinary Study of Literature,* Volume XIV, No. 1, Winter 1981, pp. 61–90.

An earlier version of chapter 3 first appeared in *Modernism: Challenges and Perspectives,* edited by Monique Chefdor, Ricardo Quinones, and Albert Wachtel, University of Illinois Press, Urbana-Champaign and Chicago, Illinois, 1986, and is reprinted here with the permission of University of Illinois Press.

Produced and distributed by
UMI Research Press
an imprint of
University Microfilms, Inc.
Ann Arbor, Michigan 48106

Library of Congress Cataloging in Publication Data

Isaak, Jo Anna.
The ruin of representation in modernist art and texts.

(Studies in the fine arts. Art theory ; no. 13)
Revision of the author's thesis (Ph.D.)—University of Toronto, 1982.
Bibliography: p.
Includes index.
1. English literature—20th century—History and criticism. 2. Modernism (Aesthetics) 3. Avant-garde (Aesthetics) 4. Joyce, James, 1882-1941—Knowledge—Art.
5. Stein, Gertrude, 1874-1946—Knowledge—Art.
6. Vorticism—Great Britain. 7. Futurism (Literary movement)—Soviet Union. 8. Art and literature.
I. Title. II. Series.
PR478.M618   1986   820'.9'1   86-19289
ISBN 0-8357-1760-7 (alk. paper)

Contents

Illustrations

1

Introduction

The relationship between painting and literature used to be considered self-evident. In the seventeenth century they were called the Sister Arts. It is still customary to use terms borrowed from art history to classify or describe certain novels, poems, or plays. But it is curious that while these general thematic or structural resemblances are taken for granted, they are so taken in a very loose metaphorical way. Terms such as "impressionist novel" or "expressionist drama" suggest, for the most part, no immediate or formative relationship with the visual arts, but only a loose analogy thought to be due primarily to the common influence exerted on both writers and painters by the general temper of their period. At the same time, while these loose analogies are common, attempts at closer comparisons between the different arts are viewed with suspicion. It is considered perfectly legitimate to point to the influence of one writer on another, or the debt of one painter to another, but few people, apparently, accept the notion that the structure and content of a writer's work might have been influenced quite directly by specific paintings, or by technical innovations and aesthetic theories current in the visual arts.

The inability of some literary scholars to deal with other arts can be exemplified by the case of one who assumed, when William Carlos Williams told him Böcklin's *Die Toteninsel* had affected him while he was writing a certain early work, that the poet must have *read* this work while studying in Germany.[1] Another scholar, in a lengthy essay on James Joyce, asserts that Joyce discovered the theory for what he calls "the new novel of simultaneity" in a preface to a novel by Karl Gutzkow called *Die Ritter vom Geiste* written in 1857.[2] He gives no evidence that Joyce ever read what he refers to as a deservedly obscure work and he acknowledges that the techniques by which the theory of simultaneity could be practised were beyond the scope of the German author. Even though this is an extremely roundabout approach to the origins of simultaneity in Joyce's *Ulysses,* most literary scholars would be more at ease with it than they would be with the notion that Joyce was influenced by the new theory of simultaneity current in the visual arts.

Even for scholars who acknowledge the connections between the arts of modernism, there is frequently a reluctance to look for specific formal influences one art form may have had upon another. Christopher Gray begins his book *Cubist Aesthetic Theories* by announcing: "Cubism was more than another artistic 'ism.' It was something much deeper. Cubism was a vital force which found expression in music and literature as well as in the visual arts of painting and sculpture."[3] In keeping with this multimedia notion of cubism, he devotes a section of his book to the cubist poets Guillaume Apollinaire and Max Jacob. Gray's discussion of these poets is limited to the aesthetic theories they have in common with cubist painters because, as he says, "The affinity between the painting and the poetry of the Cubist movement does not lie in a common technical means—for, after all, the processes of visual representation of paints cannot be directly adapted to the written word—but rather in a common set of ideas about aesthetic problems" (100). This statement, which seems so reasonable on the surface, is a curiously limited, almost dated approach to comparisons between the arts, especially when the visual aspects of the poetry Gray discusses were so important. Frequently, in his discussion of cubist poetry, Gray neglects its modern art context in favor of past literary origins. For example, he turns to baroque poetry for the origin of Apollinaire's invention of the *calligramme*. It would, in fact, be possible to go all the way back to the ancient Greeks to find instances of shaped poetry, but it would be much more to the point, in view of the radical differences between Apollinaire and either the baroque poets or the ancient Greeks, to look to the more immediate impact of the visual arts and see Apollinaire's invention as an attempt to close the gap between poetry and the visual arts. Here again is another example of a critic going far afield to find the source of new elements in a writer's work within the same medium rather than seeking it in the contemporary but separate medium.

The following discussion of the relationship between literature and art is limited to the modern period. This limitation is not arbitrary; it is based on the premise that only in the modern period—with its preoccupation with the question of form, and the various attempts to break the "laws" of aesthetic perception—is a genuine connection established between the visual and verbal arts. Without professing to establish a set of first principles or criteria of modernism, it is possible to locate within the developments of art and literature of the modern period certain salient features common to both arts and, in doing so, illuminate more fully the universe of discourse to which each belongs. The book is not designed to argue a general theory of modernism, but to represent the various elements that any interdisciplinary study will be obliged to take into account. The arrangement is primarily by areas of artistic exploration rather than by individual movements, although the focus will be on cubism, Italian futurism, dadaism, vorticism and Russian futurism and will extend at times to suprematism and constructivism. The literary exhibits will be drawn from the writings of James Joyce, Gertrude Stein, Wyndham Lewis and Victor Khlebnikov and from the aesthetic theories of T.E. Hulme, Ezra Pound and the Russian formalists. This study of the relationships between the arts of modernism is a series of essays each varied in its approach—the results of a methodological exigency adapted to the variations in modes of aesthetic production, an open enunciation of a search for the laws of each aesthetic practice, not the empirical application of a particular methodology to an indifferent object.

The Modernist Paradigm/Paradox

The chapter entitled "Joyce's *Ulysses* and the Cubist Aesthetic" considers some of the fundamental paradigms of modernism, illustrated by reference to a close reading of certain sections of *Ulysses,* particularly the Wandering Rocks episode. One of the central features of modernism is that it is an era of high aesthetic self-consciousness, and nonrepresentationalism, in which art turns from realism and humanistic representation toward style, technique or form. "No artist tolerates reality," Friedrich Nietzsche announced. The task of art is its own self-realization. Clement Greenberg gives a kind of thumbnail sketch of the abolition or deconstruction of representation in art:

> The avant-garde poet or artist tries in effect to imitate God by creating something valid solely on its own terms, in the way nature itself is valid, in the way a landscape—not its picture—is aesthetically valid; something *given,* increate, independent of meanings, similars or originals. Content is to be dissolved so completely into form that the work of art or literature cannot be reduced in whole or in part to anything not itself. . . . This is the genesis of the "abstract." In turning his attention away from subject matter of common experience, the poet or artist turns it in upon the medium of his own craft. The non-representational or "abstract," if it is to have aesthetic validity, cannot be arbitrary and accidental, but must stem from obedience to some worthy constraint or original. This constraint, once the world of common, extroverted experience has been renounced, can only be found in the very processes or disciplines by which art and literature have already imitated the former. Those themselves become the subject matter of art and literature.[4]

This attenuation of reality and aesthetic self-referentiality has often been taken as a base for a definition of modernism and has laid it open for attack, especially by certain Marxist critics such as Georg Lukács who, in his defense of nineteenth-century realism, denounces modernism as a form of late bourgeois aestheticism. On the other hand, ideologists of modernism such as Roland Barthes levy the same attack against realism. "The writing of Realism," Barthes argues, "is far from being neutral, it is on the contrary loaded with the most spectacular signs of fabrication. . . . The writing of Realism is condemned to mere description by virtue of this dualistic dogma which ordains that there shall only ever be one optimum form to 'express' a reality as inert as an object, on which the writer can have no power except through his art of arranging the signs."[5]

There is, paradoxically, another view of modernism asserted by some of its practitioners—that is, that modernism is an art not only of derealization but of intense realism—that the experiments of modernism are revolutionary probes into future human consciousness and hitherto unknown phenomena. Fredric Jameson speaks of the "twin vocations of the greatest modern writing: to forge a new language and with it to convey some hitherto unexperienced phenomena of an unfamiliar external world, as new as on the first day."[6] It is within the project of modernism that man emerges as a being *of* language, *homo pictor* or *homo significans,* a creature whose universe is increasing and who is himself being constituted by the symbols of his own making. Jameson is sceptical of what he describes as "the modernist conviction that sense perception can ultimately be fully rendered in a sentence structure, that a 'parole pleine' is possible, that the world really does exist to end up in a Book which will replace it and in which the glint of sunlight on a pond, the stir of wind upon the earth's surfaces, will thus forever gleam and mildly tremble in the eternal immobility of the printed sentence" (72). Lyotard, however, is not at all sceptical; tomorrow's encyclopedias, he suggests, may be the data bank which could become "nature" itself.[7]

Joyce's part in all of this is rather interesting; *Ulysses* is used as an exhibit of both modernist hermeticism and the culmination of realism. Joyce's *Ulysses* seems to be above all, as one critic says, the reduction of experience to expression for the sake of expression, the expression mattering more than what is being expressed. Yet Joyce said of *Ulysses,* "I want to give a picture of Dublin so complete that if the city one day disappeared from the earth it could be reconstructed out of my book." This claim for a work so little concerned with description suggests that it is not by way of description that Dublin was intended to be recreated in *Ulysses.* The only way it could be reconstructed would be through some process of distillation, whereby the fragments of the raw materials that composed the work could be extracted and reassembled. Fragmentation is one of the keys to this central aesthetic paradox of certain modernists works, that is, their nonmimetic, yet intensely realistic nature: elements of reality were incorporated into the artistic discourse, actually presented, not *re*-presented. In this Joyce finds his counterpart in the fragmentation and collage aesthetic of cubist painting and in the incorporation of random, unconscious or chance operations of the later dada and surrealists.

This same nonmimetic yet realistic intention can be argued for the break with traditional conceptions of perspective in art and the multiplication of point of view in literature. The only compositions appropriated to the new ways of seeing are those that address the new dispositions of space and time. The actual influence of Einstein's model of a non-Euclidean, four-dimensional space-time continuum, or the theories of F.H. Bradley or A.N. Whitehead, or the optical aesthetic speculation of J.H. Hildebrand and H.L.F. von Helmholtz, or the Bergsonian notion of *durée,* or even the experience of a speeding motor car upon the composition of a canvas or a novel has been debated from the time certain artists claimed some of these theories and experiences as the rationale for their compositional experiments. The subtle distortions of perspective that were the result of Cézanne's painstaking observation impressed the phenomenologist Maurice Merleau-Ponty as an almost scientific investigation of the relation between perception, time and memory. It is apparent that modernism is the art of modernization, of technology, of the new physics, of industrial acceleration—a response of the imagination to urbanization. It is the art consequent on a world reinterpreting, reinventing itself.

The development of techniques by which the notions of temporality and synchronicity could be incorporated into the visual arts (cubism, futurism, simultanism) was, in certain ways, analogous to the development of spatial form in literature. As early as 1919, in his essay on Khlebnikov, Roman Jakobson expressed the need for a critical investigation into the problem of time and space as forms of poetic language: "L'idée de l'espace comme une convention picturale, du temps idéographique, s'infiltre dans la science de l'art. Mais le problème du temps et de l'espace comme formes du langage poétique est encore étrange à la science."[8]

In 1945 Joseph Frank, in "Spatial Form in Modern Literature," argued that modern literature as a whole is engaged in a concerted effort to confute the limitations that have always been prescribed to language, in particular, the linearity of narrative sequence. Frank's essay is a central document in the context of comparative studies, for it suggests ways of investigating compositional changes in modern art as well as literature. *Spatial Form in Narrative,* edited by Jeffrey R. Smitten and Ann Daghistany, which reprints Frank's essay along with a number of other essays placing spatial form in the context of modernist aesthetics and contemporary literary theory, is witness to the ongoing critical debate that surrounds the concept of spatial form in literature.

The abolition or deconstruction of representation in art; the alteration or abrogation of certain aesthetic conventions in order to come to terms with new ways of seeing; the break with traditional conceptions of perspective in art and the multiplications of point of view in literature (what has come to be termed the polyphonic text); the aesthetic, philosophical and political implications of fragmentation and collage; the exploration of random, unconscious or chance operations: the comparative study of Joyce's *Ulysses* and the cubist aesthetic will reveal these paradigms or paradoxes of modernism. The similarities between the arts of modernism lie open and accessible, on the very surface, so to speak, of the works of art themselves. To see these connections requires only that we be as open and as flexible in our critical endeavor as the artists were in their creative one.

Runes of Representation

The English vorticists present quite different critical problems from those presented by Joyce and the early cubists. Joyce exhibited almost all the salient features of modernism, whereas the English vorticists, although they played a crucial role in the development of Anglo-American modernism, marked an independent trajectory. This is exemplified particularly in the case of Wyndham Lewis who, as Jameson describes him, was

> at one and the same time the exemplary practitioner of one of the most powerful of all modernistic styles and an aggressive ideological critic and adversary of modernism itself in all its forms. Indeed, *Time and Western Man* (1927) diagnostically attributes the aberrant impulse of all the great contemporary artistic and philosophical modernisms to what he called the "Time Cult," to the fetish of temporality and the celebration of Bergsonian flux. However illuminating this diagnosis may have been, it had the unfortunate effect of forcing his readership to choose between himself and virtually everything else (Joyce, Pound, Proust, Stein, Picasso, Stravinsky, Bergson, Whitehead, etc.) in the modern canon.[9]

The eclecticism of Wyndham Lewis's artistic activity is what brings him into this study. He saw himself as "one of those portmanteau-men of the Italian Renaissance."[10] "The Editor of this paper is a painter," Lewis announced in the preface to *The Tyro*.

> In addition to that you will see him starting a serial story in this number. During the Renaissance in Italy this duplication of activities was common enough, and no one was surprised to see a man chiselling words and stone alternately. If, as many are believing, we are at present on the threshold of a Renaissance of Art ... then the spectacle becomes so common that the aloofness of the Editor of this paper from musical composition would, retrospectively, be more surprising than his books of stories and essays.[11]

As writer, painter and founder of an art movement that offered, in Pound's phrase, "a common ground for the arts," Lewis epitomizes the tendency of the times. "For a moment in the just-before-the-war days," Ford Madox Ford recalled, "the Fine, the Plastic and the Literary Arts touched hands with an unusual intimacy and what was called oneness of purpose."[12]

In December 1910, at the beginning of this revolution in England, Arnold Bennett had foreseen the possible effect of the postimpressionist exhibition on literary artists: "I have permitted myself to suspect," Bennett wrote in *The New Age*, "that supposing some writer were to come along and do in words what these men have done in paint, I might have to begin again. This awkward experience will in all probability not happen to me, but it might happen to a writer younger than me. At any rate, it is a fine thought."[13] This same thought was occurring to a number of other writers at the time. Lewis, in fact, began his experimental writing because, as he said, his "literary contemporaries were too bookish and not keeping pace with the visual revolution."[14]

The convergence of the arts in England came to a head with the publication of the vorticist manifesto *Blast* in 1914 and the vorticist exhibition at the Dore Galleries in June 1915. Although vorticism was developed primarily by visual artists, its expressed intention was to incorporate the literary arts as well. The presence of Ezra Pound, philosopher and art critic T.E. Hulme, and sculptor and writer Henri Gaudier-Brzeska secured the position of literature within the movement. As Pound explained, "We wished a designation that would be equally applicable to a certain basis for all the arts."[15] In his essay on vorticism he stressed, "What I have said for one Vorticist art can be transposed to another Vorticist art."[16] According to Lewis, vorticism "affected equally the images which issued from its visual inspiration and likewise the rather less evident literary sources of its ebullience."[17]

T.E. Hulme, in a lecture on "Modern Art and Its Philosophy" delivered to the Quest Society in January 1914, laid the foundations for a theoretical edifice based on the new "tendency towards abstraction" that would emerge in a few months as vorticism. Hulme's vindication of abstraction, which he credited with the overthrow of representational art (what he described as the enfeebled "sloppy dregs" of a dying romanticism), was inspired by the theoretical speculations of Wilhelm Worringer's *Abstraction and Empathy: A Contribution to the Psychology of Style,* 1908. The heart of Worringer's thesis is that there are two polar aesthetic urges—to empathy and to abstraction—that are manifested in antithetical art forms, the vitalistic or naturalistic on the one hand, and the nonnaturalistic, geometric or primitive on the other. Abstract art derives from cultures that either fear nature and feel "an immense spiritual dread of space," or radically distrust nature and believe it to be an illusion:

> Tormented by the entangled inter-relationship and flux of the phenomena of the outer world, such peoples were dominated by an immense need for tranquility. The happiness they sought from art did not consist in the possibility of projecting themselves into the things of the outer world, of enjoying themselves in them but in the possibility of taking the individual thing of the external world out of its arbitrariness and seeming fortuitousness, of eternalizing it by approximation to abstract forms and, in this manner, of finding a point of tranquility and a refuge from appearances. Their most powerful urge was, so to speak, to wrest the object of the external world out of its natural context, out of the unending flux of being to purify it of all its dependence upon life, i.e. of everything about it that was arbitrary, to render it necessary and irrefragable, to approximate it to its *absolute* value.[18]

The crucial consequences of this artistic volition, Worringer goes on to argue, were on the one hand the approximation of the representation to a plane, and on the other strict suppression of the representation of three-dimensional space and the exclusive rendering of the single form:

> The artist was forced to approximate the representation to a plane because three-dimensionality, more than anything else, contradicted the apprehension of the object as a closed material individuality, since perception of three-dimensionality calls for a succession of perceptual elements that have to be combined; in this succession of elements the individuality of the object melts away. On the other hand, dimensions of depth are disclosed only through fore-shortening and shadow, so that a vigorous participation of the combinative understanding and of habituation is required for their apprehension. In both cases, therefore, the outcome is a subjective clouding of the objective fact, which the ancient cultural peoples were at pains to avoid.
>
> Suppression of representation of space was dictated by the urge to abstraction through the mere fact that it is precisely space which links things to one another, which imparts to them their relativity in the world-picture, and because space is the one thing it is impossible to individualise. In so far, therefore, as a sensuous object is still dependent upon space, it is unable to appear to us in its closed material individuality. All endeavour was therefore directed toward the single form set free from space. (21-22)

The avant-garde's interest in primitive art was given impetus and philosophical credibility once Worringer removed the connotation of "backward" from the term "primitive." Worringer's study of abstraction is a repudiation of Theodor Lipps's theory of empathy in which the art of the past was seen largely as a history of technical ability; primitive geometrical art, according to Lipps, was an inferior formula concocted by artists who lacked the talent to convey the organic lines of realistic form. However, Worringer argues that "the peculiarities of style in past eras, can be traced back, not to any deficiency in knowledge, but to a differently directed will-to-art" (15). The psychic precondition for the urge to empathy, according to Worringer, "is a happy pantheistic relationship of confidence between man and the phenomena of the external world [whereas] the urge to abstraction is the outcome of a great inner unrest inspired in man by the phenomena of the outside world" (15). He describes this state as one in which man either fears nature and feels an immense spiritual dread of space, or radically distrusts nature, is hostile to the phenomenal world and believes it to be an illusion. In either case the "will-to-art" diverges from naturalism to create forms that are characterized by an emphasis on linear-geometrical patterns, on an elimination of three-dimensional shapes and three-dimensional space and on the dominance of the plane in all types of plastic art.

However generalized and unsubstantiated Worringer's psychology of style may have been, his defense of primitive abstract art came at a crucial time in the development of vorticist and Russian futurist aesthetic theory. His ideas were disseminated in Russia by his friend Kandinsky and in England by T.E.

Hulme who, during the winter of 1911, heard Worringer lecture on art at the Berlin Aesthetic Congress. Hulme returned to England and gave the lecture on "Modern Art and Its Philosophy," in which he applied Worringer's theories about the abstract art of the so-called primitives to "the tendency towards abstraction," characteristic, Hulme said, of "the present movement in Europe."[19] Chiefly attracted to Worringer's theories by prospects of "dehumanization," Hulme directed the vorticist movement away from the Western humanistic tradition (i.e., the art that Hulme called romantic) toward the primitive plastic arts of Africa, the ideograph art of China and Japan and the highly stylized mosaic art of Byzantium. The dehumanization of art was to be "the chief diagnostic of the modern world of the machine age.... It may be objected," Lewis writes in *Blast*, "that the grandest and most majestic art in the world, however (Egyptian, Central African, American) has rather divested man of his vital plastic qualities and changed him into a more durable, imposing and in every way harder machine; and that is true."[20] Gaudier-Brzeska, in his manifesto statement, announced: "I shall derive my emotions solely from the arrangement of surfaces, I shall present my emotions by the arrangement of my surfaces, the planes, and lines by which they are defined."[21]

Hulme shortly became the chief aesthetician for the vorticists. His theories were so influential that Lewis was forced to comment: "All the best things that Hulme said about the theory of art were said about my art. We happened ... to be made for each other, as critic and 'creator'. What he said should be done, I *did*. Or it would be more exact to say that I did it, and he said it."[22] Four months after hearing Hulme's lecture, Lewis in *Blast* describes the vorticists as the "Primitive Mercenaries in the Modern World"—the war was with the "doctrines of a narrow and pedantic Realism"[23] and its complicity in the maintenance of things as they are.

Hulme's simplified but clear-cut theory, developed from elements of Worringer's thesis—the interest in primitive art, the urge to abstraction, the dehumanization of art, the movement away from the confusion of the flux, the representation of the flat plane and the suppression of the representation of space—provided some of the central tenets of the vorticist aesthetic and conferred the philosophical respectability to the movement necessary to distinguish it from the Continental avant-garde: cubism and Italian futurism. Hulme firmly refuted any supposition that he was "speaking of futurism which is, in its logical form, the exact opposite of the art I am describing, being the deification of the flux, the last efflorescence of impressionism" (91). Lewis complained to F.T. Marinetti that the futurists' depiction of bodies in motion results in a confused blur, whereas vorticism expressed itself in the classically controlled depiction of the separate, precisely defined object. In *Blasting and Bombardiering* Lewis recounts an altercation he had with Marinetti after Marinetti berated him for his lack of enthusiasm for speed and machinery:

"You have never understood your machines! You have never known the *ivresse* of travelling at a kilometer a minute. Have you ever travelled at a kilometer a minute?"
"Never." I shook my head energetically. "Never. I loathe anything that goes too quickly. If it goes too quickly, it is not there."
"It is not there!" he thundered for this had touched him on the raw. "It is *only* when it goes quickly that it *is* there!"
"That is nonsense," I said. "I cannot see a thing that is going too quickly."
"See it—see it! Why should you want to *see*?" he exclaimed. (37)

Hulme also dissociated vorticism from "certain elements of cubism, which I might call analytical cubism—the theories about interpenetration which you get in Metzinger for example" (93). Instead of interpenetrating elements, the vorticist w⸳s to focus on "one element which seems to be gradually hardening out and separating itself from the others" (94). "The new tendency towards abstraction will culminate," he continued, "not so much in the simple geometrical forms found in archaic art, but in the more complicated ones associated in our minds with the idea of machinery" (97). He praised Lewis for his paintings and drawings in which the "only interest in the human body was in a few abstract mechanical relations perceived in it, the arm as a lever and so on." Jacob Epstein, too, was commended for his drawings for sculpture, where the theme of birth and generation was transformed "into something as hard and durable as a geometrical figure itself" (97).

It was a simple matter to apply Worringer's observations to modern developments in the plastic arts, but Hulme was among the first to realize that literary form would undergo a change similar to changes in the plastic arts. The essay "Romanticism and Classicism" is Hulme's attempt to define this change as it affected literary form. It is a denunciation of romantic subjectivity, of the unrestrained emotionalism which for Hulme was the worst feature of romanticism. According to Hulme, nonnaturalistic art in its suppression of the organic also suppressed the subjective and the personal. The corresponding style in literature would also be impersonal and objective: "I prophecy that a period of dry, hard, classical verse is coming" (137). Hulme's fragmentary intuitions touched on two central issues: that the movement toward abstraction was common to both literature and the plastic arts and that the plastic arts were thought to provide (in ways as yet unclear) a resource for the overhaul of literature.

Hulme's prophecy is, in fact, an echo of one that Pound made in 1912—in a poetic credo entitled "Prolegomena" he said that the best poetry of the coming decade "will be harder and saner.... It will be as much like granite as it can be.... We will have fewer painted adjectives impeding the shock and stroke of it. At least for myself, I want it so, austere, direct, free from emotional slither."[24]

Still, how this hard, austere, unsentimental verse was to be executed remained indefinite. In 1914, however, Pound describes the creation of an outstanding early poem, called "In a Station of the Metro," in ways that were to provide a directive for the poetics to come.

> Three years ago in Paris I got out of a "metro" train at La Concorde, and saw suddenly a beautiful face, and then another and another . . . and I tried all that day to find words for what this had meant to me, and I could not find any words that seemed to me worthy, or as lovely as that sudden emotion. And that evening, as I went home along the Rue Raynouard, I was still trying and I found, suddenly, the expression. I do not mean that I found words, but there came an equation . . . not in speech, but in little splotches of color. It was just that—a "pattern," or hardly a pattern, if by "pattern" you mean something with a "repeat" in it. But it was a word, the beginning, for me, of a language in color . . . I realized quite vividly that if I were a painter, or if I had, often, *that kind* of emotion, or even if I had the energy to get paints and brushes and keep at it, I might found a new school of painting, of "non-representative" painting, a painting that would speak only by arrangements in color.[25]

If Pound really did think of language in these visual and formal terms as early as 1911, then he was among the first to do so. The "Metro" poem did not achieve its final version until two years later. The first version ran to thirty lines, the second, written six months later, was half that length. In the final version, the poem, pared down to its fundamental constituents, approaches more precisely his original idea of nonrepresentative color patches. It is just two lines:

> The apparition   of the faces   in the crowd:
> Petals   on a wet, black   bough.

The break with conventional language usage and the unexpected simplicity of juxtaposing two discrete visual images was facilitated by Pound's investigation of the ideographic use of language found in the Japanese haiku tradition. The spaces left between the words within each line—a technique rendered accurately in print only in the version of the poem published by *Poetry* in April 1913—forces the reader to perceive the poem as a visual as well as verbal entity. "In the 'Metro' hokku, I was careful, I think, to indicate spaces between the rhythmic units, and I want them observed."[26] While the poem retains the conventional semantic usage of a simile, its innovations in the disruption of conventional syntax, the montaged semiabstract images, and the exploration of the potentials of typography were to be developed into a fully articulated practice by both the vorticists and Russian futurists.

In spite of Hulme's efforts, vorticism has been analyzed repeatedly in terms of its early dependence upon cubism and futurism, with little acknowledgment of its own assertion and actualization of an independent trajectory. The movement toward abstraction took place very rapidly in England. By the time of the second *Blast* manifesto, Lewis was demanding the end to all representational art: "There should be a bill passed in Parliament at once forbidding any image or recognizable shape to be stuck up in any public place."[27] Neither Picasso or Braque was ever an abstract artist in the way that Lewis or David Bomberg or Frederick Etchells were. In part, the precociousness of abstract art in England can be accounted for by understanding the close connection between vorticism and Russian futurism.

Central to the achievement of the Russian avant-garde was the very idea of abstract art itself—of an art practice not contingent upon empirical experience, but art as process and mode of perceptual and formal experience. English vorticism and Russian futurism are linked together by their radical shifts in modes of aesthetic production, theoretical positions, treatment of perceptual and linguistic conventions, and the repudiation of their determinant role in producing representations of the ideological world for the sake of the specific materiality of the signifying practice. This study will compare some of the primary documents in which the Russian futurists and English vorticists define their goals and distinguish their art production from European avant-garde practices—particularly Marinetti's futurism. It will analyze how strategies of abstraction evolved out of a comparative investigation of linguistic and plastic media. The study will also explore the rediscovery of primitive art, which influenced the inception of abstract art both in Russia and in the West.

Unseating the Patriarchy

While the writers of the vorticist group had to struggle to dissociate themselves from traditional literary criticism and to argue the connections between their innovations and the innovations in the visual arts, Gertrude Stein's writing has never been comfortably placed within the context of any literary tradition. Its inappropriateness has prevented it from being appropriated. No literary critic has ever attempted to claim Stein's work for the canon in the way, for example, T.S. Eliot attempted to redeem Joyce's *Ulysses* for "The Great Tradition" and even for Christianity. It is this historical, original patriarchy that Stein intends to disturb:

> Patriarchal Poetry their origin and their history their history
> patriarchal poetry their origin patriarchal poetry their history
> their origin patriarchal poetry their history patriarchal poetry
> their origin patriarchal poetry their history their origin.
> That is one case.
> Able sweet and in a seat.

"The privileged moment of individualism," Michel Foucault has argued, "was the coming into being of the notion of the author."[28] The concept of the author as "origin," "father," the person having final "authority" over "meaning" is intricately tied to the confident bourgeois belief in absolute property rights. But modernity—when freed of the first author, "God"—began to disturb these virile illusions. "Paternity may be a legal fiction," Joyce speculates in an episode of *Ulysses* in which the proprietal assumptions of man, both in the act of begetting and in the act of authorship, are brought into question. "Fatherhood, in the sense of conscious begetting is unknown to man. It is founded upon the void, upon incertitude, upon unlikelihood. *Amor Matris*, subjective and objective genitive, may be the only true thing in life."[29] The death of the author has wholly different implications for those who have never acceded to this privileged position: Woman has never been "cocksure" in the same manner as credulous man. Woman's estrangement from phallogocentrism is explored in Gertrude Stein's writing, not from a restorative perspective with the aim of gaining inscription, but from the perspective of a subject who has never been inscribed. The margin is reformulated as the frontier.

The approach to be adopted in analyzing Stein's text will be based on structural and semiological theories. It will not align itself with any particular school, but will open out in a number of directions—from the theories of Ferdinand de Saussure which form the basis for most contemporary structuralists' thinking, toward the linguistic investigations of Roman Jakobson, toward Roland Barthes's analysis of the pleasure to be found in the text and toward the theoretical speculations of Julia Kristeva. Kristeva, while never addressing Stein's work, indicates why it is probably necessary to be a woman to venture such a subversion of the paternalistic symbolic order of language as Stein attempted.

I shall draw on these and other investigations concerning the possibility of a theory in the sense of an analytical discourse on signifying systems that take into account the crisis of meaning, subject and structure, precisely because it is in the confrontation with these issues that Stein's work initiates a radically new intention for the practice and function of writing. In each case the theoretical approaches have been chosen because they open consideration of the kind of interartistic experimentation characteristic of early twentieth-century artistic production; they are not methodological approaches whose applicability is unique to any particular signifying practice. The development of a semiology—a general science of signs—designed to deal with both verbal and nonverbal systems of signification, provides a nonmetaphorical vocabulary for dealing with the analogies between Stein's writing and developments in the contemporary visual arts.

The totality of Stein's work as well as the theoretical investigations brought to bear on the work may most fruitfully be seen as an attack on the presumption of "innocence" within the signifying practice. The notion that we "encode" our experience of the world in order that we may experience it, that there exists no pristine range of experience open to us, comes directly from the work of B.L. Whorf and Edward Sapir. In Sapir's classic statement, we invent the world we inhabit, we modify and reconstruct what is given:

> Human beings do not live in the objective world alone, nor alone in the world of social activity as ordinarily understood, but are very much at the mercy of the particular language which has become the medium of expression for their society. It is quite an illusion to imagine that one adjusts to reality essentially without the use of language and that language is merely an incidental means of solving specific problems of communication or reflection. The fact of the matter is that the "real world" is to a large extent built up on the language habits of the group.... We see and hear and otherwise experience very largely as we do because the language habits of our community predispose certain choices of interpretation.[30]

It follows that, implicated as we are in this gigantic, covert, collaborative enterprise, none of us can claim access to an innocent, uncoded, pure or objective experience of a real, permanently existing world. It is precisely this presumption of an innocent, uncoded world that Stein's writing dismantles.

The fundamental discoveries of modern linguistics reveal that signification, which appears to be a natural relation, is in reality an arbitrary system of difference in which elements gain their meaning only from their relation with all other elements. Saussure originated this conception of language, with its concomitant modes of study, in his lectures from 1907 to 1911, published after his death as the *Course in General Linguistics*. Saussure's definition of the sign runs as follows: "The linguistic sign unites, not a thing and a name, but a concept and an acoustic image," the latter terms being then replaced by a new set, the signified and signifier. Further, the link between the signified and signifier is wholly arbitrary; it rests entirely on social convention and acceptance and has no "natural" fitness in and of itself. The same is true for iconic sign systems, as illustrated in Umberto Eco's analysis of his drawing of a horse:

> If I take a pen and draw on a sheet of paper the silhouette of a horse, through creating this silhouette by the extension of a single, elementary line of ink, everyone will be prepared to recognize a horse in my drawing; and yet the one property which the horse in the drawing has (a continuous black line) is the sole property which the real horse *does not have*. My drawing consists of a sign, which delineates 'the space within = horse' and separates it from the 'space without = non-horse,' whereas the horse does not possess this property— therefore I have produced on my drawing *not one condition of perception;* for I perceive the horse on the basis of a large number of stimuli, not one of which is distantly comparable to an extended line.

He concludes that "Iconic signs reproduce a few conditions of perception, but only when these have been selected on the basis of codes of recognition and explained on the basis of graphic conventions."[31] Thus, the very construction of the concept of a sign severely qualifies the most archaic language theory of all, that of the indissoluble link between words and things, Cratylus's conception of language as names and naming. There can no longer be any question of such an intrinsic relationship once the arbitrary character of language and iconic sign systems has been made clear.

The opening of the famous gap between signifier and signified had a radical effect on the understanding of the operations of signifying systems. It made possible a study of the relations of the signifiers themselves in the production of meaning. The analysis of the proper relations of the signifiers led to the conclusion that no meaning is sustained by anything other than reference to other meaning. The signifier cuts out or articulates the signified only by relations entered into with other signifiers: meaning is only produced by a systematic arrangement of differences. Further, as this system of language exists prior to the individual's birth, the acquisition of a language requires that a person be subjected to its conventions. Thus, man is to be understood as constructed by the symbol and not as the point of origin of symbolic production.

Jacques Lacan's investigations provide a radically new way of situating the subject in relation to language and ideology. Freud's discoveries designating sexuality as the nexus between language and society are taken up by Lacan to illuminate the problematic of the subject in language and the structure of language in the unconscious. Freud had already suggested the applicability of linguistic analysis in the exploration of the unconscious in describing the dream as having the structure of a sentence or of a rebus; that is, it has the structure of a form of writing. Lacan's work consists of a translation of the Freudian topology into linguistic terms, so that eventually all of the apparently experimental or even existential phenomena dealt with by Freud—such as desire, anxiety, the castration complex, the Oedipal complex—will be reformable in terms of a linguistic model. This in turn suggests why, as Peter Brooks says:

> We can read Freud's *Beyond the Pleasure Principle* as a text concerning textuality, and conceive that there can be a psychoanalytic criticism of the text itself that does not become—as has usually been the case—a study of the psychogenesis of the text (the author's unconscious), the dynamics of literary response (the reader's unconscious), or the occult motivations of the characters (postulating an "unconscious" for them). It is rather the superimposition of the model of the functioning of the mental apparatus on the functioning of the text that offers the possibility of a psychoanalytic criticism. [32]

Lacan dissociates his notion of the unconscious from our image of the Freudian id:

> It's wrong to think that the unconscious exists because of the existence of unconscious desire, of some obtuse, heavy, caliban, indeed animalistic unconscious desire that rises up from the depths, that is primitive, and has to lift itself to the higher level of consciousness. Quite on the contrary, desire exists because there is unconsciousness, that is to say,

language which escapes the subject in its structure and effects, and because there is always, on the level of language, something which is beyond consciousness, and it is there that the function of desire is to be located.[33]

As Fredric Jameson explains "Psychic or affective depth is for Lacan, therefore, not located in the subject's relationship to his own inner depths (to his own unconscious or past or whatever) but, rather,... in his projective relationship to that other implied by the linguistic circuit."[34] Thus, according to Lacan's famous formula: "L'Inconscient, c'est le discours de l'autre." This discourse of the other is distinct from, but comparable in structure to the conscious language system or symbolic order in which the subject has to take up a position in order to communicate. Lacan has designated the latter as the "Name-of-the-Father," a term used to convey the notion of language as the cultural origin of law, as embodied by the myth of the father as the protagonist of the family structure whose real or imagined prohibition of incest is the first social law.

In *Revolution in Poetic Language* Julia Kristeva argues that what is repressed in the individual during the acquisition of symbolic language are the pre-Oedipal functions that connect the infant (infant meaning without speech) to the mother's body—rhythmic, preverbal, polymorphic drives that are expressed in rhyme, intonation, repetition, babble. This Kristeva calls the *le sémiotique* ("the semiotic"), which is not to be confused with semiotics, the general science of signs. The semiotic she sees as one of the components of the signifying process, the other being "the symbolic." The semiotic is never completely repressed and reappears within language as its materiality, tone, rhythm—the irruptions, the disruptions, the nonsense, the play that threatens meaning, that threatens stability. Because the semiotic is bound up with the mother's body it is closely connected with femininity, yet it arises in a stage prior to the distinctions of gender and therefore is not essentially feminine. Nevertheless, as the symbolic order (source of such fixed signs as God, father, state, order, property, propriety) is the patriarchal sexual and social order governing modern society, for the French feminist theorists associated with the polemic for female "différence" the semiotic is associated with the feminine. Both the symbolic and the semiotic are associated with a force within society that disrupts, opposes and threatens received social order. Kristeva looks to the semiotic as it appears in the avant-garde text as a means of undermining the symbolic order. "Indifferent to language, enigmatic and feminine, this space underlying the written is rhythmic, unfettered, irreducible to its intelligible verbal translation, it is musical, anterior to judgment"; it is that "air or song beneath the text" which is allied with woman.[35]

These theories, with their assertion of a radically new way of situating the human subject in relation to language and ideology, and the instability of the connection between signifier and signified, opened heretofore unknown possibilities for the analysis of the avant-garde text and, by extension, avant-garde art. The division of the Saussurean sign prevents a language or text from being reduced to one law or one meaning, and it introduced the possibility of envisioning language as a free play, without closure. It also introduced a more radical potentiality, one in which the revolutionary aspect of the avant-garde is located, since the signifier could be seen to have an active function in creating and determining the signified. These possibilities, suggested although not developed in Saussure's theories, became crucial in the exploration of the avant-garde text. The attempts by Barthes, Kristeva and others to deal with the avant-garde text demonstrated the active function of the signifier in the production of meaning. A disruption of the symbolic order of language can be understood as a revolution in the sphere of politics: "Literary practice is seen as exploration and discovery of the possibilities of language; as an activity that liberates the subject from a number of linguistic, psychic, and social networks; as a dynamism that breaks up the inertia of language habits and grants the unique possibility of studying the *becoming* of the significations of signs."[36] The link between an avant-garde literary practice and revolution may be interpreted as an affirmation of freedom, as an anarchic revolt against the reality that has already been written for us.

In *Writing Degree Zero* Barthes sketches a kind of conceptual history of literature in which the writer, in what Barthes calls the bourgeois periods (classical and romantic), has no other option but to position himself in relation to a preexistent literary tradition much as any subject must position himself in relation to a preexistent symbolic order. If, Jameson points out, "the symbolic order is the source of meaning, it is also and at the same time the source of all cliché, the very fountainhead of all those more debased 'meaning-effects' which saturate our culture."[37] This is essentially the same criticism Barthes launches against bourgeois writing. The practitioners of this style inculcated a sense of its inevitability, a sense that such a way of writing was not really a style so much as a transparency, an innocent reflection of reality. Barthes sees this attitude toward writing as a characteristic act of bourgeois expropriation, part of a grand design whereby all aspects of bourgeois life acquire the same air of naturalness, of rightness, of universality and inevitability:

> Classical language is always reducible to a persuasive continuum, it postulates the possibility of dialogue, it establishes a universe in which men are not alone, where words never have the terrible weight of things, where speech is always a meeting with others. Classical language is a bringer of euphoria because it is immediately social. There is no genre, no written work of classicism which does not suppose a collective consumption regulated by the contingencies of society.[38]

Such writing acts as the institutionalized carrier, transmitter, or encoder of the bourgeois way of life and its values. When those values disintegrate, as they began to in the mid–nineteenth century, and the writer ceases to be a witness to the universal, his first gesture, according to Barthes, is to choose the commitment of his form: "Classical writing therefore disintegrated, and the whole of literature, from Flaubert to the present day, became the problematics of language" (3).

In order not to be made a tributary of the hegemonic bourgeois order, the writer of the avant-garde text seeks to abolish the tradition in which he is enclosed. This is what Barthes calls "the zero degree of writing," the attempt to realize the Orphean dream—a writer without literature. "Without any resort to the content of the discourse and without falling back on some ideology, there is no mode of writing left, there are only styles, thanks to which man turns his back on society and confronts the world of objects without going through any of the forms of history or of social life" (52).

Barthes distinguishes between two sorts of writers: those for whom writing is instrumental, a vehicle for an ulterior purpose and who write *about* other things, and those for whom the verb "to write" is intransitive, whose central concern is not to take us "through" writing to a world beyond it, but to produce writing. A writer of the latter type is a "writer for whom language is a problem, who experiences its profundity, not its instrumentality nor its beauty."[39] He has as his field "nothing but writing itself, not as pure 'form' conceived by an aesthetic of art for art's sake, but, much more radically, as the only area [*espace*] for one who writes."[40]

Such an attitude toward language constitutes what Kristeva calls a wreckage of the paternalistic symbolic order. "When the most solid guarantee of our identity—syntax—is revealed as a limit, the entire history of the western subject and his relationship to his enunciation has come to an end."[41] Although, as she says, "We have not yet grasped the importance of a change of venue that involves thinking about the subject on the basis of literary practice rather than on the basis of neurosis or psychosis," she does begin the analysis of implications for the subject in process within an "artistic" practice (97). "'Literary' and generally 'artistic' practice transforms the dependence of the subject on the signifier into a test of its freedom in relation to the signifier and reality. It is a trial where the subject reaches both its limits (the laws of the signifier) and the objective possibilities (linguistic and historic) of their displacement" (97). Kristeva's theoretical discourse on the subject is the search for "the laws of its desire, operating as a hinge between immersion in the signifier and repudiation (it is neither one nor the other), its status unknown" (120).

Conventional criticism aims at a closure of this troubling ambiguity; it aims at an interpretation, fixing a meaning, finding a source (the author) and an ending, a closure (*the* meaning)—the reader's role is that of passive receiver of information. The avant-garde text, on the contrary, requires a new notion of the activity of reading. In *S/Z* Barthes argues that literature may be divided into that which gives the reader a role, a function, a contribution to make, and that in which the reader, "instead of functioning himself, instead of gaining access to the magic of the signifier, to the pleasure of writing, is left with no more than the poor freedom either to accept or reject the text: reading is nothing more than a referendum."[42] Here the reader is reduced to the inert consumer, and the author's role is that of producer. Literature of the second kind Barthes terms "readerly" *(lisible)*. In it the passage from signifier to signified is presumed to be clear, well worn, established and compulsory. It thus perpetuates an "established" view of reality. Literature of the first kind, which Barthes calls "writerly" *(scriptible)*, depends upon an awareness of the interrelationship of writing and reading in the production of signification. Herein lies for Barthes what he calls the *jouissance* ("bliss, ecstasy, sexual pleasure") to be found in the text.[43] "There is no other primary significatum in literary works than a certain desire: to write is a mode of Eros."[44] Paradoxically, where the readerly texts (which require no *real* reading) are often what we call "readable," writerly texts (which demand strenuous reading) are often called "unreadable." Barthes has described the experience of reading as offering two kinds of pleasure: *plaisir* ("pleasure") and *jouissance*. *Plaisir* seems to come from the more straightforward process of reading, *jouissance* from a sense of break or interruption in the text, where the orderly linguistic purpose is subverted and the reader must partake in the production of signification:

> Text of pleasure: the text that contents, fills, grants euphoria; the text that comes from culture and does not break with it, is linked to a *comfortable* practice of reading. Text of bliss: the text that imposes a state of loss, the text that discomforts (perhaps to the point of a certain boredom), unsettles the reader's historical, cultural, psychological assumptions, the consistency of his tastes, values, memories, brings to a crisis his relation with language.[45]

Kristeva makes a comparable distinction between two responses to the symbolic function of the paternal discourse: that of the rhetorician and that of the writer in the strongest sense of the word, that is one who has style:

> The rhetorician does not invent a language; fascinated by the symbolic function of paternal discourse, he seduces it in the Latin sense of the verb—he "leads it astray," inflicts it with a few anomalies generally taken from writers of the past, thus miming a father ... but not to the point of leaving cover.... The stylist's adventure is totally different, [s]he no longer needs to seduce the father by rhetorical affections. As winner of the battle, [s]he may ... assume a different discourse; neither imaginary discourse of the self, nor discourse of transcendental knowledge, but a permanent go-between from one to the other, a pulsation of sign and rhythm, of consciousness and instinctual drive.[46]

If the avant-garde text, this heterogeneous body,[47] provides meaning, identity and knowledge, it does so in a completely different way than in the Name-of-the-Father. The "pre-sentence-making disposition to rhythm, intonation, nonsense; makes nonsense abound with sense: makes (one) laugh."[48] To rediscover the intonations, scansions, repetitions, and rhythms preceding the subject's establishment within the system of language is to discover, according to Kristeva, the voiced breath that fastens us to an undifferentiated mother, a semiotic motility, a playful polysemia that is released within poetic language. The discovery-in-utterance is also at the same time an act of losing, of distancing, of separating oneself from what has been discovered, an act of *un*knowing, a diffraction, a dissolution back into an active potential. It is not the possessing or attaining of a "truth" so that it is finished, no longer to be considered, because owned and "in the bag," but the realizing of the "known" so that it becomes again the "given," thereby not arresting reflection, but renewing and stimulating it.

Faced with this poetic language that defies knowledge, one questions the possibility, or simultaneously, the legitimacy of a theoretical discourse on this practice of language whose object is precisely to break the bounding that supports the discourse of knowledge. While acknowledging that the pre-Oedipal stages are "analytically unthinkable" but not inoperative, how does one discuss them in discursive language?

> This kind of heterogeneous economy and its questionable subject-in-process thus calls for a linguistics other than the one descended from the phenomenological heavens; a linguistics capable, within its language object, of accounting for a nonetheless articulated *instinctual* drive, across and through the constitutive and insurmountable frontier of *meaning*. This instinctual drive, however, located in the matrix of the sign, refers back to an instinctual body . . . which ciphers the language with rhythmic, intonational, and other arrangements, nonreducible to the position of the transcendental ego even though always within sight of its thesis."[49]

What is necessary, Kristeva asserts, is a desire *for* language, a passion for its materiality as opposed to its transparency, in order to carry the venture to that point where abstraction is revealed as resource, as infinite potential, to that point where meaning has not yet appeared (the child), no longer is (the insane), or else functions as a restructuring (writing, art). It is also perhaps necessary, Kristeva suggests, to be a woman to attempt to take up that "exorbitant wager" of carrying the project to the outer borders of the signifying venture of men, not to renounce the discourse of knowledge but to compel it to increase its power by giving it an object beyond its limits.[50]

These, then, are the theories to be mobilized in the following study. The aim is not to interpret the texts, but on the contrary to appreciate what pluralities constitute them, to gain access to them by several entrances, none of which can be authoritatively declared to be the main one. The networks are many and they interact, based as they are on the infinite potential of the restructuring function of the aesthetic practice.

Joyce's *Ulysses* and the Cubist Aesthetic

"In your country," Mein Herr began with a startling abruptness, "what becomes of the wasted time?"

Lady Muriel looked grave. "Who can tell?" She half-whispered to herself. "All one knows is that it is gone—past recall!"

"Well, in my—I mean in a country I have visited," said the old man, "they store it up and it comes in *very* useful, years afterwards! . . . By a short and simple process—which I cannot explain to you—they store up the useless hours; and, on some occasion, when they happen to need extra time, they get them out again!"

Lewis Carroll

So he collected like a cistern in his youth the last stagnant pumpings of Victorian Anglo-Irish life. This he held steadfastly intact for fifteen years or more—then when he was ripe, as it were, he discharged it, in a dense mass, to his eternal glory. That was *Ulysses*.

Wyndham Lewis

"Painting," Joyce truculently announced to the wife of an artist, "does not interest me."[1] Critics have taken him at his word. Over and over again, as we are told of Joyce's virtuosity in the field of music, we are reminded of his ignorance of the art world. Frank Budgen's statements that Joyce was unaware of the art movements taking place around him have contributed to this commonly held belief, and Joyce's poor eyesight has gone to support it. As a consequence, aspects of Joyce's work, whose form and content may have been determined at least in part by his attempts to emulate the achievements of pictorial art, remain largely unexamined.[2]

There is no easy way to deal with the range of interests that may have helped to determine the character of so eclectic a work of art as *Ulysses*. But if, as in the case of Joyce, an artist's work is decidedly different from that of his predecessors or contemporaries, one may well look for influences that fall outside the proper sphere of his own medium. And if the innovations current in one art are so conspicuous that they make headlines in the daily press and generate waves of controversy, it is foolish not to look for repercussions in the work of the exponents of the new in other media.

Budgen asserts that Joyce knew nothing of the contemporary developments in the visual arts, not even of those that were taking place in

Zurich during his stay there—an assertion based on the premise that if Joyce had been aware of them, then Budgen, as a painter, would have known of it. We could accept this claim if it were not for the fact that Budgen at times reveals himself to be ill-acquainted with, and sometimes even hostile to, the innovations taking place in his own art. Perhaps it is Budgen's conservative attitude he attributes to Joyce when he says of the dadaists and surrealists that "it is doubtful if Joyce would have found much in their repertoire to interest him." It is hard to imagine that Joyce, who inhabited the old quarter of Zurich where the Cabaret Voltaire was located and who was a great patron of cafés, would be as ignorant of the dadaists as Budgen suggests. Zurich dada (Hugo Ball, Emmy Hennings, Jean Arp, Sophie Tauber, Richard Huelsenbeck, Tristan Tzara, Marcel Janco and later Hans Richter and Viking Eggeling) was an international, multimedia affair. It arose in 1915 when Ball opened the Cabaret Voltaire. Here on June 23, 1916, Ball recited his sound poems, or "Verse ohne Worte," in which words have no apparent denotative function. In the same year the dada review *Cabaret Voltaire* appeared, to be followed the next year by *Dada* (July 1917). Joyce was very familiar with *Littérature* (founded in 1919), the official organ of the movement. By 1920 Joyce and many of the dadaists had moved to Paris. In 1920 André Breton staged a great dada soirée at the Théâtre de l'Oeuvre, combining an art exhibition with a public reading of dadaist writings by Picabia. This same year Joyce approached the Théâtre de l'Oeuvre to arrange a performance of his play *Exiles*.[3] There are a couple of incidents in Budgen's account of his friendship with Joyce that make one wonder if it was not Joyce who was acquainting Budgen with people and events in the art world. On their first meeting Joyce initiated a conversation about the paintings of Wyndham Lewis. Unfortunately, Budgen did not know Lewis's work sufficiently well to talk about it. Some time later it was Joyce who gave Budgen a copy of Umberto Boccioni's *Technical Manifesto of Futurist Painting* (1910).

Although no record is available of the art exhibits Joyce attended, both Richard Ellmann and Stanislaus Joyce speak of Joyce visiting art galleries. Ellmann refers to an exhibit Joyce went to very late in life—obviously poor eyesight was not a deterrent. And he notes that "Joyce probably attended the important exhibition of futurism which was held in Trieste about 1908."[4] Since futurism did not exist in 1908, Ellmann is perhaps referring to the futurist manifesto and poetry presentation held on January 12, 1910 at Politeama Rossetti, Trieste. There is also the likelihood, odd as it may seem, that Joyce attended a cubist exhibition while he was in Dublin during the summer of 1912. Gertrude Stein, in her account of the cubist painter Harry Phelan Gibb, tells how Gibb, finding a couple of patrons who believed in him, went to Dublin in the summer of 1912 and "had rather an epoch-making show of his pictures there."[5] Gibb's host and admirer was Oliver St. John Gogarty, the prototype for Buck Milligan in *Ulysses*. In all probability Joyce heard of Gogarty's protégé and visited Gibb's exhibition out of curiosity. In any case, it is highly unlikely that Joyce would have been unaware of anything "epoch-making" taking place in Dublin while he was there.

Even if we allow that Joyce never attended a cubist or futurist exhibit or a dadaist performance, we do know that he was an avid newspaper reader and, what is perhaps more important, we know that he read each installment of *A Portrait of the Artist as a Young Man* as it was being serialized in *The Egoist*. When we look through the pages of this little review, we find the story of baby tuckoo and the moocow set in the midst of the furor created by the cubists and futurists. The latest activities of these artists were discussed in almost every issue of *The Egoist*: Richard Aldington discusses Marinetti's poetry readings and lectures; in an article entitled "The New Driving Force," Huntley Carter analyzes the temporal aspects of futurism; there are book reviews of Albert Gleizes and Jean Metzinger's *Du cubisme* and A.J. Eddy's *Cubists and Post-Impressionism*; Ezra Pound writes appreciatively of the work of Wyndham Lewis and the vorticists; and in "The Battle of the Cubes" and "The Cubist Room," John Cournos and Wyndham Lewis discuss the current futurist and cubist exhibits. There is also a considerable exchange with other reviews such as *Les Soirées de Paris, Der Sturm,* and *291*. This is just a sample of the attention given to current events in art by *The Egoist*. Joyce need only have read the works which surrounded his own novel to be acquainted with the new aesthetic theories. A look at some of the major tenets of cubist aesthetics will show how closely they correspond to Joyce's own preoccupations.

The Ineluctable Temporality of the Visible

The most radical of these aesthetic theories is first articulated by Stephen, Joyce's major exponent of aesthetics. In *Stephen Hero* Stephen attacks the distinctions between the arts that Lessing makes in *Laocoön*: "The treatises which were recommended to him he found valueless and trifling; the *Laocoön* of Lessing irritated him. He wondered how the world could accept as valuable contributions such fanciful generalizations."[6] The generalization that Stephen takes issue with is Lessing's argument that painting and sculpture are essentially spatial forms and therefore static, whereas poetry is temporal, a realization of sequence in time, and therefore dynamic. In *A Portrait of the Artist as a Young Man,* Stephen argues for the apprehension of the underlying wholeness, the *integritas,* of the aesthetic image which transcends such spatial or temporal limitations.

Lessing's *Laocoön* was written as a corrective to the then common discussions about the link between the arts. It is rare to read through a critical treatise on either art or literature written between the middle of the sixteenth and the middle of the eighteenth century without finding some discussion of the Horatian simile, "as is painting, so is poetry" (*ut pictura poesis*); or, if the mention is not of Horace, then it is of the equivalent saying of Simonides that "painting is mute poetry, and poetry a speaking picture." Commentary generally centered on two popular artistic genres: pictorial poetry and allegorical painting. The pictorial poet tried to paint with words, the allegorical painter to tell a story in visual images. The failure of those attempts to overcome the essential differences in media was first systematically analyzed by Lessing in 1766.[7]

Lessing's argument originates from the simple observation that literature and the plastic arts, working through different media, must therefore differ in the fundamental laws governing their creation. Form in the plastic arts, according to Lessing, is necessarily spatial. Literature, on the other hand, makes use of language, composed of a succession of words proceeding through time, and is necessarily sequential. Lessing's attempt to clarify the confusion of genres and establish their unalterable separateness did not result in an immediate cessation of descriptive poetry or allegorical painting, but it did undermine the notion that a bridge between the arts could be established simply by analyzing similarities in theme. It is not until the modern period that the distinctions Lessing makes between the arts began to be questioned. Time and space were the two extremes defining the limits of literature and the pictorial arts; and it is possible to trace the evolution of modern art forms through their oscillations between these two poles.

Stephen's disagreement with Lessing is crucial, for it is in the attempt to overcome the intrinsic limitations of their media, as delineated by Lessing, that certain of the pictorial and the verbal arts of the twentieth century have established a genuine connection with each other—a connection not limited to anything so superficial as similarities in subject matter, but which affects the form of both arts. Wassily Kandinsky, while urging a closer relationship between the arts, had warned that "Comparison of means among the arts and the learning of one art from another can only be successful when the application of the lesson is fundamental. One art must learn how another uses its *method,* so that its own means may then be used according to the same fundamental principles, but in its own medium. The artist must not forget that each means implies its proper application, and that it is for him to discover this application."[8]

Perhaps the first critic to articulate the nature of the new form evolving in modern literature is Joseph Frank. In "Spatial Form in Modern Literature," Frank attempts to show that modern literature—exemplified by such writers as T.S. Eliot, Ezra Pound, Marcel Proust and James Joyce—is moving in the direction of spatial form. Frank's thesis is that modern literature as a whole is engaged in a concerted effort to break through the limitations that have always been prescribed to language. Frank begins his analysis of the development of spatial form with a discussion of the imagist movement. He sees Ezra Pound's definition of an image—"that which presents an intellectual and emotional complex in an instant of time"—as fundamentally important for any discussion of modern literary form:

> [A]n image is defined not as a pictorial reproduction, but as a unification of disparate ideas and emotions into a complex presented spatially in an instant of time. Such a complex is not to proceed discursively, according to the laws of language, but is rather to strike the reader's sensibility with an instantaneous impact. Pound stresses this aspect by adding, in a later passage, that only the instantaneous presentation of such complexes gives "that sense of sudden liberation; that sense of freedom from time limits and space limits; that sense of sudden growth, which we experience in the presence of the greatest works of art."[9]

This is a direct parallel to Stephen's argument for the apprehension of the underlying wholeness, the *integritas* of the aesthetic image which transcends spatial or temporal limitations. "At the very outset," Frank observes, "modern poetry championed a poetic method in direct contradiction to the way in which Lessing had said language must be perceived."[10]

The visual arts were also growing restive under Lessing's strictures. The sculptor Naum Gabo reiterates Stephen's complaint against Lessing in "The Realistic Manifesto" of 1920: "We renounce the thousand-year-old delusion in art that held the static rhythms as the only elements of the plastic and pictorial arts. We affirm in those arts a new element, the kinetic rhythms, as the basic forms of our perception of real time."[11] A parallel can be drawn between the developing spatial form of modern literature and certain trends in the visual arts. In cubism and futurism particularly, there is a similar attempt to overcome the inherent limitations of the media. In this case it is the spatial limitations of painting which are to be overcome by the incorporation of temporal elements.

The new time concept in cubist painting is a much discussed and very thorny issue among art historians. The debated issue is whether or not the cubists were consciously trying to represent pictorially the new theories of time and space that were being, or had been, developed in the field of physics by G.F.B. Riemann, Albert Einstein, and H. Minkowski. The idea that cubism was representing what was popularly known as the fourth dimension was asserted by Guillaume Apollinaire in a lecture in 1911 and in his book on cubist painters.[12] This was not the earliest mention of the fourth dimension in relation to painting. There is a little-known article by the American artist Max Weber published in *Camera Work* in 1910, entitled "The Fourth Dimension from a Plastic Point of View."[13] Weber lived in Paris from 1905 to 1908 and knew Picasso and others of his circle. The article, written two years after Weber's return to America, represents concepts to which he had been introduced while in Paris.

Jean Metzinger also related the temporal aspect of cubist art to the new theory of relativity. He suggested that previous movements in art could be correlated with scientific theories of their period and that once a particular art movement is viewed in that context it would no longer remain unintelligible. Once the apparent deformations of cubism are seen in relation to the theory of relativity, then "the fact of moving around an object to seize several successive appearances, which, fused in a single image, reconstitute it in time, will no longer make thoughtful people indignant."[14] What Metzinger seems to be echoing here is Einstein's statement that "the description of an event will vary according to the position and relative motion of the observer."[15] Metzinger's idea was to use the new physics to justify the cubist method by arguing that cubism, while apparently "irrelevant to reality," did, in fact, present a truer picture of things because it presented time as the new theories did, as a dimension of space. Though some scholars today consider these theories to be attempts on the part of the painters and their literary apologists to give their preoccupations an aura of legitimacy, these theories are representative of the interpretive notions of the time.[16]

Undoubtedly the cubists were engaged with much more rudimentary concepts than those being formulated by Einstein and other mathematicians. Leo Stein describes the effects of Picasso's meeting with Maurice Princet, who introduced Picasso and his friends to some of the current discoveries in physics and mathematics:

> There was a friend of the Montmartre crowd, interested in mathematics, who talked about infinities and fourth dimensions. Picasso began to have opinions on what was and what was not real, though as he understood nothing of these matters the opinions were childishly silly. He would stand before a Cézanne or a Renoir picture and say contemptuously, 'Is that a nose? No, this is a nose', and then he would draw a pyramidal diagram with two circles connected by crossed lines. . . . He was bent now on doing something important—reality was important whatever else it might be, and so Picasso was off.[17]

What Picasso assimilated from these discussions may indeed be reductive, although the conclusions were far from being "childishly silly." It is likely that these simplifications were the stuff paintings were made of or at least explained by, rather than any more abstruse speculation on the nature of non-Euclidean geometry.

The conviction with which Picasso asserted these opinions may be accounted for by the fact that he had access to them much earlier from his friend Alfred Jarry. Roger Shattuck speaks of the special fascination Jarry exercised over Picasso, and observed that "Among these youthful champions of the twentieth century, in the cubist doctrine they devised, and in the other isms that followed, Jarry found his progeny."[18] Certainly there is much that would interest the early cubists in Jarry's book *Exploits and Opinions of Doctor Faustroll Pataphysician: A Neo Scientific Novel.* This book was written in 1898 but not published until 1911, at which time Apollinaire hailed it as the year's most important publication. After Jarry's death in 1907, Picasso inherited his unpublished manuscripts. Pertinent to our discussion here is Dr. Faustroll's question: "Why should anyone claim that the shape of a watch is round—a manifestly false proposition—since it appears in profile as a narrow rectangular construction, elliptic on three sides; and why the devil should one have noticed its shape only at the moment of looking at the time?"[19]

There is as well as these scientific theories, a much more instinctive or visceral way of accounting for the multiple perspectives in early cubist paintings. Much credibility can be granted to the argument that early analytic cubism is a direct evolution from the later works of Cézanne. The subtle distortions of perspective resulting from Cézanne's painstaking observation impressed the phenomenologist Maurice Merleau-Ponty as an almost scientific investigation of the relation between perception, time and memory:

> By remaining faithful to the phenomena in his investigations of perspective, Cézanne discovered what recent psychologists have come to formulate: that lived perspective, that which we actually perceive, is not a geometric or photographic one. The objects we see close at hand appear smaller, those far away seem larger than they do in a photograph. . . . To say that a circle seen obliquely is seen as an ellipse is to substitute for our actual perception what we would see if we were cameras: in reality we see a form which oscillates around the ellipse without being an ellipse . . . it is Cézanne's genius that when the overall composition of the picture is seen globally, perspectival distortions are no longer visible in their own right but rather contribute, as they do in natural vision, to the impression of an emerging order, of an object in the act of appearing, organizing itself before our very eyes.[20]

Whatever the source of inspiration for the radical change that took place in Braque's and Picasso's paintings—whether the new theories in physics, the bizarre and provocative discussions with Alfred Jarry, the optical and aesthetic speculations of Hildebrand and Helmholtz, or the later works of Cézanne—it meant the abolition of the conventional Renaissance perspective which had largely persisted in Western art until cubism. Renaissance perspective presupposes a static universe. No temporal relationship is assumed to exist between the beholder and the painting; the spectator is denied movement in that the picture is viewed from one particular point. Similarly, the potentially mobile objects of the picture are arrested. Cubist pictoral space, on the other hand, suggests the addition of the dimension of time to spatial dimensions, since objects are given not as seen at any one moment, but in temporal sequence; that is, to perceive the many views of the object as given would either have required movement by the viewer through temporally sequential positions or movement on the part of the objects depicted. Braque, in describing his method of composition says that "the fragmentation [of objects] enabled me to establish space and movement within space."[21]

Futurism elaborated on the time concept in cubism.[22] The attempt to circumvent the static limitations of their medium was one of the central aims of the futurists. Boccioni, in his *Technical Manifesto of Futurist Painting* (1910), writes: "Action, in our works, will no longer be an arrested movement of universal dynamism. It will be, simply, dynamic sensation itself. Everything moves, everything runs, everything turns swiftly. The figure in front of us never is still, but ceaselessly appears and disappears."[23]

The attempt to incorporate the temporal dimension in painting and the movement toward spatial form in literature can be seen as correlative tendencies in the evolution of Western art. It is this attempt to break down the barriers of their respective media that forms the basis of the close relationship that developed between modern art and modern literature.

Through the Cracked Looking Glass

The break with Renaissance perspective in painting had a definite parallel in the treatment of point of view in modern literature. It is in the treatment of point of view that *Ulysses* differs most markedly from preceding novels— those of Henry James, for example. In the preface to *The Portrait of a Lady,* James suggests analogies between the art of the novelist and that of the painter. Using terminology taken from the visual arts, he discusses such common problems as the location of the central figure, the scale upon which other figures are to be drawn, the treatment of perspective, the composition of the background, and even the colors and light to be used. The analogies he suggests are not gratuitous; rather they are a recognition of the actual similarities between the two arts.[24] But the art to which James refers in the preface, written in 1908, is not the art of the avant-garde. It is an essentially conservative art. His determination to "leave no pretext for saying that anything is out of line, scale or perspective" suggests that he is still working within the conventions of Renaissance perspective. Yet, he recognizes its limitations. He looks out of his house of fiction through numerous windows over the human scene. Despite the choice of windows, he complains: "They are but windows at the best, mere holes in a dead wall, disconnected, perched aloft; they are not hinged doors opening straight upon life."

Although James was referring to point of view in the novel, he was also articulating the limitations of Renaissance perspective in painting. The futurists echoed James's complaint, announcing in the catalogue to the exhibition that opened at Bernheim-Jeune in 1912: "We must show the invisible which stirs and lives beyond densities, that which we have to our right, left, and behind us, and not just the little square of life artificially enclosed as though framed by the wings of a stage."[25] In "The Space-Time Concept in the Work of Picasso," Paul Laporte notes that "The epoch from Giotto to Cézanne was united in one particular aspect: the beholder was excluded from the space presented in the picture. The frame was a window opening into a space never to be reached. If the spectator was invited to enter at all he could do so only by imaginatively projecting himself into it."[26] But with the advent of "the first Cubist painting," Picasso's *Les Demoiselles d'Avignon* (figure 1), Laporte claims the relationship of spectator and painting underwent a radical change. The unity of the picture, famous for its internal stylistic disruptions, resides in the viewer's seeing himself in the same space as the figures in the painting.

In an article provocatively titled "The Philosophical Brothel," Leo Steinberg discusses further this new role of the observer: "In the *Demoiselles* painting the rule of traditional narrative art yields to an anti-narrative counter-principle: neighboring figures share neither a common action, do not communicate or interact, but relate singly, directly to the spectator."[27] This, he points out, is very different from the effect of such a picture as Rembrandt's *Syndics of the Drapers' Guild* (figure 2), where the figures gathered around a table were obviously engaged in a discussion until intruded upon. They look expectantly toward us. Although the attention of the figures in the painting is focused upon the viewer, no attempt is made to incorporate the viewer into the pictorial space itself. The figures, situated in their own unified three-dimensional space and transfixed in a moment of time, exclude us. In Picasso's *Demoiselles,* on the other hand, Steinberg points out we are not only looked at, we are invited in. The lack of a coherent unified spatial structure within the picture opens the possibility of incorporating the external spatial structure. We are shown a profile nose on a frontal view of the face, and the back as well as the face of the seated figure, thus disrupting the internal spatial relationship. The table seems to be invading the picture from the space occupied by the viewer. The absence of rapport between the figures, their mutual autonomy and dissociation even from their own doings, and their incapacity for joint participation in a unified space—all these "negative" factors heighten the positive hold of each figure on the responsive viewer.

What occurs in Picasso's paintings as a result of multiplying the perspectives later became a conscious aim on the part of futurists. "Painters have always shown us things and persons in front of us," said Umberto Boccioni. "We shall place the spectator at the center of the picture."[28] In this way cubism changed the status of the easel picture, which had always been isolated from the world about it, much as Henry James complained the

Figure 1. Pablo Picasso, *Les Demoiselles d'Avignon,* 1907
Oil on canvas, 244 × 233 cm.
(Collection, The Museum of Modern Art, New York.
Acquired through the Lillie P. Bliss Bequest)

Figure 2. Rembrandt Hermanszoon van Rijn, *Syndics of the Drapers' Guild (The Staalmeesters)*, 1661–62 189 × 280 cm. (Rijksmuseum-Stichtung, Amsterdam)

traditional novel was isolated from "life." Catching the spirit of the movement, Gertrude Stein announced that

> because the way of living had changed, the composition had extended and each thing was as important as any other thing . . . the framing of life, the need that a picture exist in its frame, remain in its frame was over. A picture remaining in its frame was a thing that always had existed and now pictures commenced to want to leave their frames and this also created the necessity for Cubism.[29]

The new aesthetic, which was developing a new role for art, also required a new role for the artist. For the work of art to have an immediate relationship with external reality the artist had to give up his traditional role of middleman between his work and its audience. Joyce's categories of lyrical, epical, or dramatic art depend upon how immediately the work relates to its audience: "the lyrical form (is) the form wherein the artist presents his image in *immediate relation to himself*; the epical form the form wherein he presents his image in *mediate relation to himself and to others*; the dramatic form, the form wherein he presents his image in *immediate relation to others*." Joyce reserves the highest praise for the dramatic: "The esthetic image in the dramatic form is life purified and reprojected from the human imagination, the mystery of esthetic like that of material creation is accomplished. The artist, like the God of the creation, remains within or behind or beyond or above his handiwork, invisible, refined out of existence, indifferent, paring his fingernails."[30] The artist, instead of presenting his single point of view, was to maintain a kind of neutrality by presenting multiple points of view, and this in turn altered the relationship of the audience and the work of art.

Julia Kristeva analyzes this phenomenon—what she calls the polyphonic text—in her discussion of Mikhail Bakhtin's study of Dostoevsky. "The polyphonic novel which Bakhtin finds in Dostoevsky's work [Joyce is cited as another example] is built on that breach of the 'I' caused by the explosion of modern literature: a plurality of languages, a confrontation of types of discourse and ideologies, with no conclusion and no synthesis—without 'monologic' or any axial point."[31] The polyphonic text shatters the ideological identity of the utterance of the text in general, that is, the construction of a single ideology. "A text is not ideological, according to Bakhtin, unless it rests on 'the unity of a mind', the unity of a speaking 'I', which guarantees the validity of an ideology. . . . Now in the polyphonic text the ideologies are shaped by the discourse of the divided speaker: they are fragmented and spread through the inter-textual space. . . . " Instead of presenting a single ideology the polyphonic writer *"prepares confrontations* (of points of view, of minds, of voices, of texts)." This in turn has a further consequence:

In such a rhetorical disappearance of the subject-speaker and of the objectality (material or ideological), Bakhtin uncovers something he cannot put a name to: the crumbling away of the representational system. This is precisely what the terms "dialogic" and polyphonic come to suggest, contrasted with the "monologic" as the token of representational discourse. (114)

The old concept of novel as mirror no longer obtains; instead, as Kristeva puts it, we move "through the looking-glass" and are engaged in what "takes place behind the mirror." What she describes as Bakhtin's concept of the new role of the reader is a direct parallel to Steinberg's theory of the viewer of Picasso's *Demoiselles.* The polyphonic text "destroys the monologic of representational literary discourse and sets the general scene for a kaleidoscopic and pluralistic way of writing in which we see nothing, for it is the writing which sees us" (115).

The Abnihilization of the Etym

Fragmentation is one of the most familiar characteristics of twentieth-century art: Yeats's reference to our pluralistic world as one in which "the centre cannot hold" has become a cliché. But for the most part the modern artist is not concerned with things holding, for holding implies stasis. He is not interested in the perfect, static state of being, but rather in the eternal dynamism of becoming which inevitably involves destruction. "In the old days," Picasso explains, "pictures went forward towards completion by stages. Every day brought something new. A picture used to be a sum of additions. In my case a picture is a sum of destructions. I do a picture—then I destroy it. In the end though, nothing is lost...."[32] The continuous dissection and reconstitution of forms, referred to in *Stephen Hero* as the modern spirit of "vivisection," is the essential process by which multiple point of view is achieved in the cubist work of art. This vivisection is fully realized in *Ulysses,* where the world of appearances is continuously being broken up into fragments and reconstituted.

Fragmentation is the key to one of the central aesthetic paradoxes in certain works of modern art and literature—its nonmimetic, yet intensely realistic nature. The construction of *Ulysses* illustrates the paradox. "I want," Joyce told a friend, "to give a picture of Dublin so complete that if the city one day suddenly disappeared from the earth it could be reconstructed out of my book."[33] But it was not by way of description that Dublin was recreated in *Ulysses.* The only way it could be reconstructed would be through some process of distillation whereby the raw materials that Joyce used for the work of art could be extracted. Like the cubist painter, Joyce was investigating the multiple *uses* of actuality. He clung tenaciously to every particle of reality that his publishers, afraid of libel suits, wanted to edit. In literature as in art, the intention was to incorporate as much of reality as possible, without perpetuating the illusion that reality was being imitated.

Robert Rosenblum, in outlining the basic tenets of cubism, explains this paradox for both art and literature: "Instead of assuming that the work of art was an illusion of a reality that lay beyond it, Cubism proposed that the work of art was itself a reality that represented the very process by which nature is transformed into art."[34] The elements of reality are fragmented and reshuffled so that new forms may come into being. Apollinaire noted that "Picasso gives an enumeration so complete and so decisive of the various elements which make up the object that these do not take the shape of the object." He goes on to say that this new art "does not dispense with the observation of nature, and acts upon us as intimately as nature herself."[35] The last phrase is particularly important. The cubists saw their paintings as constructed objects having their own independent existence, self-contained worlds, not reflecting the outside world but recreating it in a completely new form. They analyzed the world, then formally composed it again to compete with actuality, to raise the tension between the material and its representation. Braque, we are told, was fond of taking his canvases out into the fields to have them "meet" things—not to see how accurately his paintings imitated reality, but to see how well they could *compete*: *"One must not imitate what one wants to create."*[36] In a similar manner Stephen Dedalus, in his role as artist, thinks of himself as "a lord and giver of life" and as the "conscious rational reagent between a micro and macrocosm ineluctably constructed upon the incertitude of the void."[37]

The break with certain mimetic conventions in literature took place in a manner similar to that of painting. The images of a poem, like the iconographic elements in a painting, were no longer used simply for their referential value. The image did not have to "mean" something or refer to something in the outside world; it was allowed its own independent existence within the context of the poem. The step from the concept to the thing itself, from the image as metaphor to the image as subject was accomplished by the same process of fragmentation. Bram Dijkstra's account of this process in the poetry of William Carlos Williams could readily be applied to Joyce:

> What Williams tried to do . . . was to isolate aspects of the visual world, and combine them in such a manner that what was sequential in the world of physical existence became instantaneous in the work of art derived from it. This he achieved through a redistribution of the forms of nature, which, in turn, he effected by rearranging the traditional lines of experience until they accorded with the constructs of his imagination. Thus the reader is presented with a new aspect of reality which intensifies the emotive power of the experience in question, because the sentence and image fragmentation, which in writing inevitably result from such a procedure, approximate far more closely than a conventionally

structured piece of writing the constructs of the poet's creative imagination (which Williams took to be a mental kaleidoscope consisting of old and new images, whole objects, and fragments of last year's as well as yesterday's experiences.) Sentence and image fragmentation, which make a poem into a "canvas of broken parts," became basic features of Williams' poetry.[38]

Spaces of Time through Times of Space

Although the early cubists rejected the unified perspective of classical art, they were still concerned with creating the illusion of depth. The problem was solved, at least partially, by repudiating the opacity of solid objects.[39] Transparencies of objects in the foreground could be superimposed upon objects in the background, thereby enabling the cubist to incorporate into his flat two-dimensional design objects visible in a three-dimensional depth perspective. This telescoping of planes and interpenetration of form unite nearness and distance. In descriptions of landscape, Joyce evokes a kind of flat perspective that might be compared with perspective in a landscape by Braque—as, for example, in the following: "Signs on a white field. Somewhere to someone in your flutiest voice. The good bishop of Cloyne took the veil of the temple out of his shovel hat: veil of space with colored emblems hatched on its field. Hold hard. Colored on a flat: yes, that's right. Flat, I see, then think distance, near, far, flat I see, east, back. Ah, see now. Falls back suddenly, frozen in stereoscope" (*U,* 48). "Stereoscopic" is an appropriate term for this cubist technique, whereby multiple pictures of an object taken from different points of view (in this case planes of view) are put together to produce the effect of a three-dimensional object in space. In the passage cited Joyce describes one of the cubist techniques of composition perhaps more accurately, certainly more vividly, than the cubists describe it themselves.

The technique of superimposition can best be applied to the temporal aspect of the novel. As Budgen points out, "Joyce with his own material can do what no painter can within the limits of color and flat surface. He can build up his picture of many superimposed planes of time."[40] Take, for example, this short paragraph from the Sirens episode:

> Tenors get women by the score. Increase their flow. Throw flowers at his feet when will we meet? My head it simply. Jingle all delighted. He can't sing for tall hats. Your head it simply swirls. Perfumed for him. What perfume does your wife? I want to know. Jing. Stop. Knock. Last look at mirror always before she answers the door. The hall. There? How do you? I do well. There? What? Phila of cachous, kissing comfits, in her satchel. Yes? Hands felt for the opulent. Alas! The voice rose, sighing, changed: loud, full shining, proud. (*U,* 274)

Bloom is listening to the tenor voice of Simon Dedalus and reflecting upon the sexual prowess of tenors. Interpolated into this reflection are excerpts from a song that Milly's letter brought to his mind earlier in the morning, a comment about Blazes Boylan's singing ability, a question from Martha's letter, and a couple of "jingles" which throughout the novel have served to indicate the whereabouts of Blazes Boylan, who is now on his way to Molly. The passage ends with Bloom envisioning what will happen when Boylan arrives. In this way we are given simultaneously not only what is going on now and what has gone on at different intervals earlier in the day, but also what is going on in another location and what is about to go on there. Numerous planes of space and time have been superimposed. What distinguishes this technique from the common novelistic technique of flashback is that Joyce, concerned with surface and texture, is not so much interested in entering the past as he is in having segments of the past (or the future) overlap upon the present.

The Wandering Rocks

Budgen relates that Joyce once asked if the Cyclops episode struck him as being futuristic. According to Armin Arnold, this query indicates that Joyce "evidently had no idea what Marinetti and his followers were, in fact, preaching."[41] But if we put this question in the context of another conversation about the Cyclops episode we begin to doubt Arnold's assessment. While planning and composing the episode Joyce reread Swift. He complained to Budgen that "Swift treated the giant-dwarf theme a little too simply. He just multiplies or divides by twelve, and forgets that when you multiply or divide you create another organism. There must be a relative difference of speed, resistance to air pressure, and so on."[42] Such problems Swift could ignore, but the artist—even the literary artist—working in the age of Marinetti could not.

Budgen's response to Joyce's question was to say that the Cyclops episode was cubist rather than futurist: "Every event is a many-sided object. You first state one view of it and then you draw it from another angle to another scale, and both aspects lie side by side in the same picture."[43] But the episode that is most cubist in its nature is not the Cyclops, but the Wandering Rocks. For it is here that Joyce most fully utilizes the new language of discontinuous planes and masses, and we are introduced to a world in which the fixed and the absolute are replaced by the indeterminate and relative.

The textual planes of the Wandering Rocks chapter, superimposed, slip behind and within each other, plane intersecting narrative plane in bewildering reflexive interchange. The viewpoint changes from one sentence to another so that the reader must be continually on the alert to follow the variations of scale and angle of vision. We shift from a close-up to a bird's-eye view, from an external to an internal perspective, from Thornton's fruit shop to the Merchant's Arch, from the Dedalus home to Dillon's auction rooms. Scenes pile on top of one another and exist simultaneously in the same place. When we are about to find our bearings the scene shifts—another adjustment of tonality, plane and rhythm.

The episode seems almost to be an exercise in proving Whitehead's hypothesis that an event is only a manifold of relationships determined by one's point of view. Each event in the chapter is reiterated in numerous different contexts, and as the context is altered the event is also altered. The most obvious example is the progress of the one-legged sailor. He is introduced in the first section when Father Conmee gives him his blessing but not his silver crown; in the second section a coin is flung to him from a window in Eccles street while "Corny Kelleher sped a silent jet of hayjuice arching from his mouth" (*U,* 225); at the start of the third section the sailor is just rounding MacConnel's corner, having not yet reached Eccles street, and at the end of this section we read:

> The gay sweet chirping whistling within went on a bar or two, ceased, the blind of the window was drawn aside. A card *Unfurnished Apartments* slipped from the sash and fell. A plump bare generous arm shone, was seen, held forth from a white petticoat bodice and taut shiftstraps. A woman's hand flung forth a coin over the area railings. It fell on the path. (*U,* 225–26)

Father Conmee, at this point, even though we had already followed him to Malahide Road in the first section, is back traveling on the Dolymount tram.

A single event is presented several times, and with each presentation the sequence of events is altered as the point of view changes. Viewed from one position the jet of hayjuice arches from Corny Kelleher's mouth at the same time the coin is flung from the window, but from a different point of view the coin is flung after Corny Kelleher spits. Father Conmee may be disrupting lovers in a field when the sailor receives the coin, but, depending upon the point of view of the observer, the priest may still be traveling on the Dolymount tram—such are the mysteries of the relativity of time.

All these events occur within the first three sections. But it is not until what seems to have been a considerable lapse of time that this sequence of events is finally completed. In the ninth section, Lenehan, while walking along Wellington Quay, relates to M'Coy his story of the Glencree dinner, which Molly Bloom attended. The tale is interrupted momentarily as we read: "A card *Unfurnished Apartments* reappeared on the windowsash of number 7 Eccles street" (*U,* 234). Molly's gesture of replacing the card serves to synchronize the events of four sections and stretches a moment of time across some ten pages of text. What seems like confusion on the narrative plane is the logical result of multiplying the points of view. Such ubiquity permits Joyce to unite persons and moments that appear to be widely separated. It gives a strange transparency to his scenes, since we perceive their principal elements through varying exposures.

Near the close of the first section, when Father Conmee encounters a young couple emerging from a gap in the hedge, "the young man raised his cap abruptly: the young woman abruptly bent and with slow care detached from her light skirt a clinging twig" (*U,* 224). A fragment of this episode—the close-up of the girl's self-conscious action—we later find interjected into Ned Lambert's description of the Reverend Hugh C. Love. Again, in the eighth section, while Ned Lambert conducts the Reverend Mr. Love over the ancient site of the council chamber of Saint Mary's Abbey, a piece from the sixteenth section is inserted: "From a long face a beard and gaze hung on a chessboard" (*U,* 230). Buck Mulligan puts the pieces together later when he explains that the face belongs to Parnell's brother, who is playing chess in the Dublin Bakery Company's restaurant.

For the Wandering Rocks to become intelligible we are required to read it in a way comparable to the way we would "read" a cubist painting. We must be able to recognize the scattered fragments and attempt to reassemble them while keeping in mind the numerous contexts in which the parts were found and the multiple ways in which the pieces interlock.

The examples looked at so far are among the least complex of the fragmentations and interpolations found in the chapter. We can distinguish the characters or events mentioned relatively easily because we are given a substantial amount of information about them. Often, though, the fragments are so small, the information given so slight and so piecemeal that the task of reconstruction becomes extremely complex. There are characters in the Wandering Rocks chapter who are presented to us only as a rustling skirt, a disembodied smile, a beard, a back, a distant silhouette, a set of false teeth. It is only with considerable effort that we are able to fit the pieces together. Take, for example, the case of a character I will call the "dark lady." While Father Conmee is in the midst of his thoughts about old times in the barony and the fate of the first countess of Belvedere, we are told that a "listless lady no more young, walked along the shore of Lough Ennel" (*U,* 223). Father Conmee's thoughts about the countess are then superimposed upon the image of the "listless lady": "Mary, first countess of Belvedere, listlessly walking in the evening, not startled when an otter plunged," And in the ninth section, interjected into Tom Rochford's account of his machine, we read:

> Lawyers of the past, haughty, pleading, beheld pass from the consolidated taxing office to Nisi Prius court Richie Goulding carrying the costbag of Goulding, Collis and Ward and heard rustling from the admiralty division of King's bench to the court of appeal an elderly female with false teeth smiling incredulously and a black silk skirt of great amplitude. (*U,* 232)

At first we have no reason to suspect any relationship between these two women—the overlapping bits of information are too slight. But in the tenth section, the two figures whom we assumed to be separate merge into one when we are told that "an elderly female, no more young, left the building of the courts of chancery, King's bench..."(*U*, 236). The same lady with some variation in her smile is found again in the last section: "Past Richmond bridge at the doorstep of the office of Reuben J. Dodd, solicitor, agent for the Patriotic Insurance Company, an elderly female about to enter changed her plan and retracing her steps by King's windows smiled credulously on the representative of His Majesty" (*U*, 252). Our lady, or parts of her, may appear elsewhere as well but the fragments are too small or too scattered for us to recognize her.

Not only are figures fragmented and dispersed in the way they would be on a cubist canvas, they are also multiplied and presented from different angles simultaneously by reflection and refraction. Young Patrick Dignam stops to look at a poster in the window of Madame Doyle, court milliner. "From the sidemirrors two mourning Masters Dignam gaped silently.... Master Dignam on his left turned as he turned. That's me in the mourning.... He turned to the right and on his right Master Dignam turned, his cap awry, his collar sticking up" (*U*, 250). In this way we are shown not one, but three Masters Dignam. Similarly, Mr. Powers finds himself speaking to "the stalwart back of Long John Fanning ascending towards Long John Fanning in the mirror" (*U*, 247). Again, as Mr. Kernan walks along James street he finds his own image in the mirror of Peter Kennedy, hairdresser. The figure he sees there is that of a stylishly dressed, handsome young man: "High color, of course, Grizzled moustache. Returned Indian officer" (*U*, 240). This reflected image is distorted, for when we are shown the original it turns out to be "a stumpy body...on spatted feet" (*U*, 240). Perhaps because Mr. Kernan is so easily deceived by illusions created by reflected images he is momentarily deluded into believing he sees Ned Lambert's brother: "Is that Lambert's brother over the way, Sam? What? Yes. He's as like it as damn it. No. The windscreen of that motorcar in the sun there. Just a flash like that. Damn like him" (*U*, 240).

The closing section of the Wandering Rocks chapter differs from its beginning in that the fragmentation of objects and events becomes progressively minute, which in turn causes the narrative tempo to speed up. The chapter opens with the long, relatively uninterrupted account of Father Conmee's progress through Dublin. But as the chapter continues the number of interjections increases, as do the allusions to incidents in previous sections, until, in the final section, the narrative has become so fragmented that no one view is sustained for more than a few sentences. As the fragmentation increases so does the momentum, until in the end the scenes whirl before us at a breakneck pace. Here, in this last section, Joyce has achieved the literary representation of that universal dynamism Boccioni called upon artists to portray:

> Everything moves, everything runs, everything turns swiftly. The figure in front of us never is still, but ceaselessly appears and disappears... objects in motion are multiplied and distorted, following one another like waves through space....
> The sixteen persons traveling with you in a streetcar are one, ten, four, three. They sit still and they move. They come and go; they bounce into the street, are devoured by a sunlit patch, then return to their seats in front of you, persistent symbols of universal vibration. Sometimes on the cheek of the person we are talking to we see a horse passing far away. Our bodies enter into seats; the streetcar that is passing enters into the houses, and the houses in turn hurl themselves onto the streetcar and merge with it.[44]

As we ride the streetcar with Father Conmee, catch fleeting glimpses of objects and parts of people, see three Masters Dignam, a distorted Mr. Kernan, and Lambert's brother in the windscreen of a motor car in the sun, we can see how closely Boccioni's manifesto, a text Joyce used for his Italian lessons, relates to the construction of this episode.

Polysemous Polyphony

By utilizing techniques of cubist and futurist art—by incorporating the combination of elements brought about by the superimposition of various planes, combining the close with the distant observation, multiplying the possible spatial relationships of the objects represented and conveying a sense of universal dynamism—Joyce is able to create what J. Mitchell Morse calls the new novel of simultaneity, in which the traditional order of events— sequence and causal relationship—is suspended.

According to Morse, the theory that underlies the novel of simultaneity was first outlined by Karl Gutzkow in the preface to his *Die Ritter vom Geiste* (1850 to 1857). There is no evidence that Joyce ever read this obscure work, however, and Morse's claim that the theoretical preface influenced Joyce becomes especially tenuous when we realize that while Joyce was writing *Ulysses* simultaneity was a common topic of discussion in artistic journals, including *The Egoist*.[45] In *Les Soirées de Paris,* Apollinaire traced the development of the idea of simultaneity from Picasso, Braque and Léger to the futurists who extended it into a full-blown aesthetic theory.[46] Marcel Duchamp and Francis Picabia explored the boundaries of simultaneity, and Robert Delaunay was declared its champion when he made it the basis of his aesthetics. Delaunay claimed simultaneity to be the new element in all the arts.

Simultaneity soon became an "ism" in its own right, and various branches of simultaneity evolved, from Delaunay's simultaneous color contrasts to the futurists' simultaneity of states of mind. The simplest definition of simultanism and the one most pertinent to our investigation here is given in *291*:

> The idea of simultanism is expressed in painting by the simultaneous representation of the different figures of a form seen from different points of view, as Picasso and Braque did some time ago; or by the simultaneous representation of the figure of several forms as the futurists are doing.
>
> In literature the idea is expressed by the polyphony of simultaneous voices which say different things. Of course, printing is not an adequate medium, for succession in this medium is unavoidable and a phonograph is more suitable.
>
> That the idea of simultanism is essentially naturalistic is obvious; that the polyphony of interwoven sounds and meanings has a decided effect upon our senses is unquestionable, and that we can get at the spirit of things through this system is demonstrable.[47]

This definition precedes a literary example of simultanism presenting snatches of overheard conversation and then the directive that "all these phrases must be uttered simultaneously."

There are much more sophisticated versions of simultaneity in literature than the example in *291*. The *Ulysses* passages examined earlier are much better examples, as are Joyce's portmanteau phrases in *Finnegans Wake,* every word of which is an intersection of multidimensional meaning. Also, Pound's use of the ideogram is a means of achieving simultaneity with language; "that is to say it is one idea set on top of another," Pound explains. For those writers more closely associated with the painters, attempts to overcome verbal successiveness quickly took them into the realm of the visual. The most famous example is Blaise Cendrars and Sonia Delaunay's "first simultaneous book" *Prose du Transsibérien* (figure 3), in which the sense of simultaneity is conveyed in many ways. The speed of the train helps break down the old unities of space and time, the experiences involved are of present sensations and past memories, and the verbal movement of the poem was given a color accompaniment based on Delaunay's theory of "simultaneous contrasts." The whole poem is designed to unfold as a continuous script—a single visual experience fusing color and words.

Signatures of All Things

The active borrowing of the actual elements of each other's medium that went on between art and literature is undoubtedly the most tangible expression of their closeness. The borrowing from other media was a conscious policy with the futurists. "There is no fear more stupid than that which makes us afraid to go beyond the bounds of the art we are practicing," announced Marinetti. "There is no such thing as painting, sculpture, music, or poetry; there is only

Figure 3. *Prose du Transsibérien et de la petite Jehanne de France,* 1914
Poem by Blaise Cendrars, "simultaneous"
illustrations by Sonia Delaunay
(Published by *Les Hommes nouveaux,* Paris, 1914;
© A.D.A.G.P., Paris/V.A.G.A., New York, 1986)

creation!"[48] In 1912 Marinetti published his theory of "free-word" poetry, in which evocative words printed in varying type faces and sizes, linked by mathematical signs rather than grammatical connectives, were scattered dramatically over the page. The painters drew upon this idea and used words in their paintings for their forms and as evocations of sounds and extrapictorial associations. Ardengo Soffici, in his *Ball of the Pederasts* (figure 4), exploited not only the visual and the auditory possibilities of the letters and words, but their poetic function as *parole in libertà* as well. This painting probably initiated the development of the *dipinto parolibero* (free-word painting) of 1914. An example of this is Carrà's *Dipinto parolibero— Manifestazione interventista* (figure 5), which is a spiral of words used to convey "the plastic abstraction of civic tumult."[49]

Apollinaire in his *Calligrammes* (1913–16) experimented with the plastic potential of typography, but he did not develop it beyond the stage of figurative representation of theme, with the result that the structure is obviously imposed on the poem. If the poem is about rain, the words are arranged in five oblique lines. Before him, in Stéphane Mallarmé's *Un Coup de dés,* the spatial field across which the poet casts his words is neither gratuitous or irrelevant as it is in traditional verse, but must be understood to be an integral part of the poem itself, in the same way that silence forms an essential part of a musical composition. Mallarmé discusses the layout of *Un Coup de dés* in the preface:

> The whites in fact, assume importance, make the first impression; the versification requires this, as ordinarily, silence around a lyric work. . . . The literary advantage of this copied distance which mentally separates groups of words or words among themselves, seems to accelerate and slow up the movement, scanning it, even imitating it according to a *simultaneous* view of the page. The theme will come forth and will vanish, quickly, according to the movement of the writing, around the fragmentary interruptions of a capital phrase introduced by the title and continued. Everything takes place by abridgement, hypothetically; one *avoids the narration.* In addition, the unadorned thought with contractions, prolongations, evasions, or its very design, results, for whoever wishes to read aloud, in a score. The difference in the type between the major motif, and secondary and adjacent ones, prescribes its importance in the delivery; and the stanza, in the middle, upper, or lower position on the page, will indicate whether the intonation rises or falls. In its elementary stage, only certain daring directions, infringements, etc., forming the counterpoint of this prosody, exist with a work which lacks precedents.[50]

In "Mallarmé: The Transcendence of Language and the Aesthetics of the Book," Gerald Brun argues that Mallarmé's ultimate purpose was "to liberate poetic language" from the "mediating function of 'ordinary speech'" which must bridge the gap between "the world of things and the universe of meaning."[51]

In "Picasso and the Typography of Cubism," Robert Rosenblum points out that collage and *papier collé,* which have often been referred to as visual

Figure 4. Ardengo Soffici, *Ballo dei pederasti (Dinamismo plastico),* 1913
Destroyed

Figure 5. Carlo D. Carrà, *Dipinto parolibero—Manifestazione interventista,* 1914
Papier collé, 18 × 29.5 cm.
(Courtesy of Dr. Gianni Mattioli)

puns, are in fact puns on the literal, verbal level as well. His essay illustrates the abundance of word play in Picasso's paintings. "Picasso," he comments, "was a member of that literary generation which included the greatest punster in the history of Western literature, James Joyce."[52] Conversely, Joyce could be described as a member of the pictorial generation that included Picasso. With the inclusion of such details as boldface newspaper headings, or a single letter that occupies an entire page, or the pamphlet advertising the coming of Alexander Dowie, which occasionally interpolates its gratuitous passage of newsprint or the letters H, E, L, Y and apostrophe S which weave throughout the novel on sandwich boards, *Ulysses* offers all the simulated textures of such paintings as Picasso's *"Ma Jolie"* (figure 6) with its stenciled letters, or Juan Gris's *Glasses and Newspaper* (figure 7), which uses fragments of newsprint.

In his poem "Zone" (1912), Apollinaire suggests a new resource for poetic material: "Handbills catalogues advertisements that sing overhead / furnish your morning's poetry for prose there are newspapers / Dime detective novels...." This is exactly the material Joyce used in the making of *Ulysses*. Herbert Gorman relates that while Joyce was writing *Ulysses* he plagued his aunt for "a great bundle of tram tickets, advertisements, handbills, posters, newspapers, programmes, city maps, all the small flotsam that daily covered the fluctuating waters of the dancing sea that was Dublin."[53] According to Rosenblum—and his observation holds true for literature as well—"the Cubist sensibility to the kaleidoscopic assault of words and advertising images to be found in the most commonplace urban situations represents the first full-scale absorption into high art of the typographical environment of our century."[54]

This desire to render the reality of the modern urban scene is only one explanation for the exchange of materials. Another is that the materials themselves were granted a new autonomy. The forms in painting were freed of their representational function; color, given its independence, need no longer coincide with form and was not restricted to the natural color of the object. Braque explained that he was "always very occupied and preoccupied with the material. I prepare my own colors.... I work with the material, not with ideas."[55] Picabia spoke of "forms and colors freed from their sensory attributes: a painting based on pure invention and recreating the world of forms according to its own desires, its own imagination."[56] Similarly, words, whether on a canvas or a page, were composed of letters that had form in space, and these forms could be manipulated. Recognizing the parallel between the cubists' use of typography and the new visual symbols they invented for depicting three-dimensional objects on the two-dimensional canvas, i.e., the small, many-faceted planes, Robert Rosenblum writes: "Confronted with these various alphabetical, numerical, and musical symbols, one realizes that the arcs and planes that surround them are also to

Figure 6.   Pablo Picasso, *"Ma Jolie" (Woman with Guitar),*
1911–12
Oil on canvas, 100 × 65.3 cm.
(Collection, The Museum of Modern Art, New York.
Acquired through the Lillie P. Bliss Bequest)

Figure 7. Juan Gris, *Glasses and Newspaper,* 1914
Gouache, conte crayon and chalk on paper and canvas,
61 × 38 cm.
(Smith College Museum of Art, Northampton, Mass.
Gift of Joseph Brummer)

be read as symbols, and that they are no more to be considered the visual counterpart of reality than a word is to be considered identical with the thing to which it refers."[57] Joyce's skill in dissecting words and forming new ones is similarly not limited to the meaning conveyed by words but extends to their tangible aspects as well.[58]

William Carlos Williams points out that just as "the painters following Cézanne began to talk of sheer paint: a picture a matter of pigments upon a piece of cloth stretched on a frame," poets began to talk of a "progression from the concept, the thought, to the poem itself." It is the taking of that step

> to come over into the tactile qualities, the words themselves beyond the mere thought expressed that distinguishes the modern, or distinguished the modern of that time from the period before the turn of the century. And it is the reason why painting and the poem became so closely allied at that time. It was the work of the painters following Cézanne and the Impressionists that, critically, opened up the age of Stein, Joyce and a good many others."[59]

This Vast Inelegance

Two final points of comparison between the arts raise broader political and philosophical questions. William Barrett—whose chapter on modern art in *Irrational Man* is a central document in this context—refers to what he calls the "flattening out of climaxes" that takes place in modern art.[60] No beginning, middle, end—such is the seeming absence of structure in *Ulysses*; and analogously, in cubist painting, there is no clearly demarcated foreground, middleground or background. The abolition of the idea of pictorial climax means that not only is the subject distributed over the canvas, but space, as well as solid form, is treated as if it had positive material existence. It is modulated with color in the same manner as material form, and is made to interpenetrate actual forms in such a way that the two often become indistinguishable.[61] In *Ulysses* the seemingly empty spaces, those in which we have only trivial events, are treated with the same care and detail as the more dramatic events: the episode in which Bloom gets breakfast and feeds the cat or the time he spends in the jakes is narrated with the same close attention as the episode in which he wins his victory over the Citizen. Formally speaking, the spirit of this art is anticlimactic.

The canon of intelligible literary structure—beginning, middle, and end—arose in a culture in which the universe too was believed to be an ordered structure, a rational and intelligible whole. The apparent chaos of much modern literature is attributable to the artist's material, to a new understanding of life itself. Thus we have a novel in which the reader will find none of the gratification to be had from sham temporality and causality, falsely certain description, clear story. The *new* novel, Alain Robbe-Grillet explains, "repeats itself, bisects itself, modifies itself, contradicts itself, without even accumulating enough bulk to constitute a past—and thus a 'story' in the traditional sense of the word."[62] Numerous critics have complained that in the course of the hundreds of pages of *Ulysses*—783 in the Random House edition—nothing happens. Actually a number of what would traditionally be considered important events occur in the course of this day, but they do not take place in conventional novelistic form. Events are not directly narrated; we have to determine their structure ourselves from nonsequential fragments of information. In this way the critical events in *Ulysses,* like the "climaxes" of a cubist painting, are diffused throughout the work.

Closely related to this reorientation of the formal structure of modern art is a reorientation of the value structure inherent in the art. Barrett points out that Western man's hierarchical view of the universe imposed a similar hierarchical view upon art. The emergence of genre painting in the seventeenth century and the rise of the novel in the eighteenth century were the first steps toward a democratization of the arts. It was not until the twentieth century, however, that the reversal of Western values was really accomplished. In *Ulysses* Joyce inverts both scale and value: to reduce the decade of the *Odyssey* to eighteen hours in the life of a man—and of an ordinary man to whom nothing happens save the most ordinary events—is perhaps one of the greatest feats of democratization in the history of Western art. Similarly, with the cubists' incorporation of mechanically reproducible items such as newspaper clippings, printed cigarette packages and bottle labels, the "fine art" of painting draws upon the warehouse of mass cultural cliché, of advertisement, of technology—ultimately it enters the street.

"Many individuals would be sensitive to the beauty of common objects, without artistic intention," Fernand Léger wrote in *The Aesthetic of the Machine,* "if the preconceived notion of the objet d'art were not a bandage over their eyes. . . . Beauty is everywhere, in the arrangements of your pots and pans, on the white wall of your kitchen, more perhaps than in your eighteenth-century salon or in the official museum."[63] This shift in values was taken to its logical extreme by the "scrap-structure" of Kurt Schwitters's *Merz* paintings and poems, by Duchamp with his "Ready-mades" and by the surrealist René Magritte, who in his *Les Valeurs personelles* (figure 8) painted the interior of a bedroom in which such commonplace objects as a pocket comb, a shaving brush, a bar of soap and a glass are the central objects of attention and are drawn on the same scale as the bed. (In this we are reminded of the bar of soap in Bloom's pocket, which is seen as capable at certain moments of taking on a transcendental importance.) Beginning with the cubists and the futurists, the categories of small or large, important or banal, even beautiful or ugly—the whole notion of what could be inserted into the aesthetic discourse—

Figure 8. René Magritte, *Les Valeurs personnelles*, 1952
Oil on canvas, 78 × 96 cm.
(© Estate of Magritte, 1986)

underwent a radical change. "Modern artists have discovered ugliness as a condition of vitality in art," announced a review in *The Egoist*. Unlike Arnold Hauser, who considers the "ugliness" of modern art to be an expression of aesthetic nihilism, a form of defeatism,[64] the artists of this scrap-structure were motivated by the recognition that inversion of traditional values allows for an expansion of our view of the world, opening our eyes to the rejected elements of existence. "Who is the genius who will tell us a legend more ravishing than this prosaic tale which is called life?"[65] asked Gabo, in *The Realistic Manifesto* of 1920. Almost as if in answer, Joyce published *Ulysses* two years later.

3

The Revolution of a Poetics

Soleil, prends garde de toi!
A.P. Wiertz

I fear we are not getting rid of God because we still believe in grammar.
Nietzsche

"What strikes me as beautiful, what I should like to do," Flaubert wrote, "is a book without external attachments, which would hold itself together by itself through the internal force of its style." Flaubert's dream of an order in art independent of the humanistic, the material, the real, was actualized in the development of abstractionism in the early 1900s when art took to analyzing its own ontology. The movements that follow Flaubert's imperative in creating art not contingent upon empirical experience but art as process and mode of perceptual and formal experience have one characteristic in common—their strategies of abstraction evolved out of a complex nexus of linguistic and plastic media. It is as though what Roman Jakobson refers to as the "bared medium" could only be realized by investigating the devices of the *other* media. In particular, strikingly similar traits can be observed among the group of English vorticists associated with Ezra Pound, Wyndham Lewis and the manifesto *Blast* (1914)[1] and the group of Russian futurists, an alliance of writers and painters who displayed a comparable urge to write manifestos that would function as *A Slap in the Face to Public Taste* (1912).[2] In the *Blast* manifesto, Pound attempted to delineate what he called the "ancestry" of vorticism by quoting Walter Pater's famous phrase on the etiological nature of abstraction in art: "all arts approach the condition of music." In the same chapter of *The Renaissance,* Pater goes on to make two other much more explicit statements. The first is that "Art is always striving to become a matter of pure perception, to get rid of its responsibilities to its *subject.*" The second describes abstraction in one medium as capable of suggesting a means of aesthetic autonomy in another. Pater notes that

in its special mode of handling its given material, each art may be observed to pass into the condition of some other art, by what German critics term an *Anders-streben*—a partial alienation from its own limitations, through which the arts are able, not indeed to supply the place of each other, but reciprocally to lend each other new forces.[3]

The Russian futurists developed the notion of the autonomy of the artistic material into a fully articulated aesthetic. Kazimir Malevich's assertion that the object of painting was the expression of the "body as such" ("The idea is to combine the variety and multiplicity of lines, space, surface, color and texture into one body as such"),[4] had its direct linguistic counterpart in Victor Khlebnikov's and Aleksei Kruchenykh's insistence on the idea of the "word as such,"[5] the self-sufficient word, free of its referent. Just as all the other arts consist in the shaping of self-validating material, so too does poetry: its "material" is words—thus poetry is characterized as obeying immanent laws, and its semantic function is reduced to a minimum. "Before us there was no art of the word," Kruchenykh wrote in *The Three* (1913), and he asserted the autonomous value of the "autotelic word." The raw material of literature was to be allowed to stand by itself, no longer chained in slavery to meaning, philosophy, psychology and reason: "The word is broader than its meaning. Each letter, each sound has its relevance. . . . Why not repudiate meaning and write with word-ideas that are freely created? We do not need intermediaries—symbols, thought, *we give our new truth and we do not serve as the reflections of some sun.*"[6] And Benedikt Livshits wrote that now poetry was "free from the sad necessity of expressing the logical connection of ideas."[7] In 1911 Pound had launched a comparable attack against the burden of reference imposed upon poetry. He complained that for over two hundred years poetry in English "had been merely the vehicle . . . the ox-cart and post-chaise for transmitting thoughts poetic or otherwise."[8]

The assertion of the right to an autonomous or autotelic aesthetic praxis should not be understood as synonymous with the solipsistic principle of "art for art's sake," but rather should be accompanied by Roman Jakobson's qualification:

> Of late criticism thinks it fashionable to stress the uncertainty of what is called the formalist science of literature. It seems that this school does not understand the relations between art and social life, it seems that it promotes *l'art pour l'art* and proceeds in the wake of Kantian aesthetics. The critics who make these objections are, in their radicalism, so consistent and so precipitate that they forget the existence of the third dimension, they see everything in the same plane. Neither Tynyanov, nor Mukarovsky, nor Shklovsky, nor I have preached that art is sufficient unto itself; on the contrary, we show that art is part of the social edifice, a component correlating with the others, a variable component, since the sphere of art and its relationship with other sectors of the social structure ceaselessly changes dialectically. *What we stress is not a separation of art, but the autonomy of the aesthetic function.*
>
> I have already said that the content of the notion of *poetry* was unstable and varied over time, but the poetic function, *poeticalness,* as the formalists stressed, is an element *sui generis,* an element that cannot be mechanically reduced to other elements. This element must be laid bare and its independence stressed, as the technical devices of cubist paintings, for example, are laid bare and independent. . . .
>
> But how is poeticalness manifested? In that the word is felt as a word and not as a mere substitute for the named object or as an explosion of emotion. In that the words and their syntax, their signification, their external and internal form are not indifferent indices of reality, but have their own weight and their own value.[9]

Make It New

As the manifesto titles suggest (*Blast, A Slap in the Face to Public Taste*), it is by way of reaction against the pluralism of bourgeois taste that these artists posit their stylistic dissent. The formal revolution—the radical shifts in modes of aesthetic production, theoretical positions, and treatment of perceptual and linguistic conventions—is the pretext for hurling a Promethean challenge, repudiating their determinate role in producing representations of the ideological world. According to André Malraux, the modern artist ventured into the field of abstractionism with the intention of escaping the hegemony and homogeneity of that "museum without walls" in which he had found himself since photographic reproduction provided the technology of pluralism—the immediate assimilation and dissemination of the work of art. Although I do not agree with Malraux's teleology of abstract art, what is important in his observation is the implied intentionality of abstractionism as reaction against the dominance of now easily reproduced "high art"— traditional academic culture which provides a fictitious, but authoritative universality and continuity with the past—and against mass culture, which is wholly attenuated from any culture created by the people, but which is "art" produced and packaged for the masses. Edmund Wilson has given these two types paradoxically contrasting names: classics and commercials.

The most famous apostle of the creed of the "classics" is T.S. Eliot who, in appropriating mythified cultural fragments to shore against his ruin, attempted to appropriate the work of Ezra Pound and James Joyce and to marshal them under the retrospective utopian banner of new literary classicism. "It is simply a way of controlling, of ordering, of giving a shape and a significance to the immense panorama of futility and anarchy which is contemporary history," Eliot writes in *"Ulysses,* Order, and Myth." This is perhaps the most candid revelation of the true compensatory impulse behind the eclectic historicist's static notion of history which enables him to create a false synthesis of cultural fragments and endow them with notions of grandeur, nobility, universality, authority—all the old verities no longer to be found in the modern world, but which, we are asked to believe, obtained in the past. The mythic method, Eliot claims, is a step toward "making the modern world possible for art."[10] In the *Slap in the Face* manifesto, this mode of artistic production, along with Pushkin, Dostoyevsky, Tolstoy et al., is the first to be thrown overboard from the "Ship of Modernity," a reaction analogous to Pound's assertion that you need not read Shakespeare, you could find out all you needed to know about him from "boring circumjacent conversation.... Better mendacities than the classic in paraphrase."[11]

The greatest adman of the "commercials" is F.T. Marinetti who, in his zeal for "the new," heroically and hysterically attempted to acculturate the entire avant-garde to the modes of production and theoretical positions of commodity capitalism in order to develop devices that would facilitate the swift communication of propaganda for that thoroughly modern merry-go-round—reification. This is borne out in Marinetti's adulation of all forms of capitalist technology and in the way in which he attempted to convert all the proponents of the Italian futurist movement into propagandists for Mussolini's Fascism.

The ostensibly dissimilar artistic or pseudoartistic production practices of mass culture and high art converge on the level of the common cult of the cliché.[12] For Pound, whose *Make It New* [13] poetics is shared by the Russian futurists who used the same slogan, Marinetti's futurism is "only an accelerated sort of impressionism,"[14] implying that it is only a new form of mimeticism. But as Jakobson maintains, "poetry is renewed from within, by specifically linguistic means," and he treats poetic language throughout his essay of *Modern Russian Poetry* (1919) as a kind of metalanguage.[15] Like Pound, who asserted that "A work of art has in it no idea which is separable from the form,"[16] Jakobson, too, denies the distinct existence of subject matter or "content." Analyses of innovations based upon external or social causation are therefore erroneous. Both Pound and Jakobson fault Marinetti for the way he directs poetry to the task of recording new facts in the material world: rapid transit, speeding motor cars, locomotives, airplanes. "But this is a reform in the field of reportage, not in poetic language," Jakobson observes and contrasts Marinetti's new mimeticism with Kruchenykh's assertion that "It is not new subject matter that defines genuine innovation. Once there is new form, it follows that there is new content; form thus conditions content. Our creative shaping of speech throws everything into a new light."[17]

Thus Marinetti's futurism and Eliot's neoclassicism, the symbolic modes of concrete anticipation and the allegorical modes of internalized cultural retrospection—are understood to be comparable devices of stultification which reinforce and reinvent the cultural power structure. They are the aesthetic manifestations of the psychic mechanisms of anticipation and melancholy. At the origin of the allegorical is an enforced and incapacitating melancholy, the result of prohibition and repression; at the origin of the valorization of manifestations of reactionary power and of reification are the continual generation and denial of expectations. When Pound, in an interview in Mayakovsky's magazine, *The Archer* (*Strelets*, 1915), disassociates himself from Italian futurism, he does so in a way that specifically addresses these ideologically induced psychic states and the manner in which they thwart the development of any genuinely innovative artistic activity capable of critical negativity:

We are "vorticists."... Everything that has been created by nature and culture is for us a general chaos which we pierce with our vortex. We do not deny the past—we don't remember it. It is distant and thus sentimental. For the artist and the poet it is a means to divert the instinct of melancholy which hinders pure art. But the future is just as distant as the past, and thus also sentimental. It is a diversion of optimism which is just as pernicious in art as melancholy. The past and the future are two brothels created by nature. Art is periods of flight from these brothels, periods of sanctity. We are not futurists: the past and the future merge for us in their sentimental remoteness, in their projections onto an obscured and impotent perception. Art lives only by means of the present—but only that present which is not subject to nature, which does not suck up to life, limiting itself to perceptions of the existent, but rather creates from itself a new, living abstraction . . . our task is to "dehumanize" the contemporary world; the established forms of the human body and all that is "mere life" have now lost their former significance. One must create new abstractions, bring together new masses, bring out of oneself a new reality.[18]

Strategies of Abstraction

Concomitant with this insistence on the new, the present, so central to both Russian futurism and English vorticism, is their interest in primitive and folk art. It is important to the understanding of neoprimitivism's entry into the avant-garde to realize that the interest inhered in the abstract form of primitive art. Primitivism, particularly as it was employed by the Russian futurists and subsequently by the English vorticists, was one of the major strategies to facilitate the creation of the autonomous, autotelic work of art.

In Pound's statements in Mayakovsky's magazine, there is an allusion to primitivism in the echoes of Nietzsche's *Der Wille zur Macht* (1901), which contains numerous statements such as: "the 'savage' person is . . . a recovery from the sickness of 'culture.' . . . Problem: where are the barbarians of the twentieth century?"[19] More explicitly, the *Blast* manifesto includes excerpts from *Concerning the Spiritual in Art* (1912), in which Kandinsky relates primitivism to abstractionism: "The more abstract the form, the more purely and therefore the more primitively it will resound." The primitive, moreover, is seen as a paradigm for artists working toward "objectivity of form, construction for the purpose of composition."[20] A few months prior to the *Blast* manifesto, both Pound and Gaudier-Brzeska had written articles aligning the contemporary and the primitive artist's drive toward abstraction. Pound's essay "The New Sculpture" was basically an attempt to remove the work of Jacob Epstein and Gaudier-Brzeska from the whole Western humanist tradition and to locate it in the context of primitive art. He claimed that "This sculpture has no relation to classic Greek, but . . . is continuing the tradition of the barbaric peoples of the earth (for whom we have sympathy and admiration)."[21] Gaudier-Brzeska, at this time, was working on his hieratic, austerely simplified *Bust of Ezra Pound* (1914), which overtly shows the influences of the powerful prehistoric art from Easter Island collected at the British Museum (figures 9 and 10).[22]

In Russia, primitivism existed as a vital artistic force between about 1908 and 1913. Vladimir Markov, in *Russian Futurism: A History,* makes a case for primitivism's being the formative aesthetic of Russian futurism. Markov

Figure 9.   Henri Gaudier-Brzeska, *Bust of Ezra Pound*
Marble, 92 × 45 cm.
(The Tate Gallery, London)

Figure 10. Anon., *Hoa-Haka-Nana-Ia (Breaking Waves),* detail
Stone, 244 × 106.5 × 56 cm.
(The Trustees of the British Museum, London)

argues that despite the group's enthusiasm for the newly found cubism, "Hylaea" (the name used for more than two years before the term futurist was adopted) did not mean cubism at all, but primitivism.[23] Russian neo-primitivism was launched in December 1909, with the Third Exhibition of the Golden Fleece. The primitivist elements in the works of this exhibition are a complex mixture of fauve-derived boldness of line, and nonrepresentational use of color as reflected in the directness and simplicity of national folk and "exotic" primitive art traditions—the appreciation of which had probably been learned, at least in part, from Gauguin and Matisse. (Larionov had been to Paris in 1906 and seen the Gauguin retrospective.) The folk art elements included an adaptation of ancient Scythian sculptures, the local vernacular painting of primitive signboards, semiabstract, highly stylized embroidery patterns from Siberia, icon painting, and the lubok (peasant woodcuts similar to English chapbooks). The interest in primitive and folk art was fueled by Russian nationalist sentiments and disseminated by retrospective utopian endeavors such as those of Savva Mamontov and Princess Mariya Tenisheva who, influenced by the English "arts and crafts" movement, established art colonies on their estates where artists were to examine and imitate local primitive art forms. The bright colors, "deliberate simplification and vulgarization of form"[24] and the immediately apparent vitality of folk art had an obvious appeal to an avant-garde bogged down in what Diaghileff termed the "weary wisdom" of late symbolism.[25]

Russian neoprimitivism was to have considerable influence on the inception of abstract art in England. Although ostensibly it arose in Russia out of nationalist sentiments and the need for a viable indigenous art form to posit in opposition to the insurgents of Western culture, it was precisely the folk or primitive aspect of Russian art that found the most favorable reception in the West—in fact, it was what the West demanded. Diaghileff's first ballet performed in the West was criticized in the French press for its lack of national atmosphere: "The French desired a folk-lore element, expected a special, almost exotic flavour in the performances. In short, they wanted what they, as Frenchmen, understood to be 'du vrai Russe.'"[26] It was in response to this demand that Diaghileff launched the *L'Oiseau de feu* (1910)—a colorful collection of various Russian fairy and folk tales. It was exactly what was called for, and by 1911 the influence of the *Ballets-Russes* spread far beyond the confines of the London and Paris elite. How great this influence was may be judged by the following extract from "Painters and the *Ballets-Russes*" by André Varnod: "It was a perfect enthusiasm which, sweeping away the artistic, literary and social worlds, reached the man in the street, the wide public, the gown-shops and stores. The fashion in everything was *Ballets-Russes*. There was not a middle-class home without its green and orange cushions on a black carpet."[27] In 1913 Diaghileff very shrewdly enlisted the talents of Natalya Goncharova. In spite of Larionov's manifesto declaration of 1913 that "we are against the West, vulgarizing our Oriental forms and rendering everything valueless,"[28] by 1914 Goncharova had impressed Paris and London as the creator of the decor of the *Coq d'or*—and Larionov too had begun to work for Diaghileff.

The appropriation by the West of ancient Russian art cannot be attributed wholly to Diaghileff's cultural transportations. T.E. Hulme's complaint about the way in which "elements taken from the extremely intense and serious Byzantine art are used in an entirely meaningless and pointless way"[29] was a response to the Byzantine-style screens, rugs, inlaid tables and paintings that proliferated in the wake of the Bloomsbury group's visit to Constantinople in 1911. Roger Fry's enthusiasm for the art he saw while on this trip may have resulted in his decision to include the work of Russian artists in his Second Post-Impressionist Exhibition (1912). Here the works of Nikolai Roerich, Mikalojus Ciurlianis, Natalya Goncharova, Mikhail Larionov and other Russian artists of what the catalogue referred to as the "New Byzantine Group" were exhibited together with the works of Vanessa Bell, Frederick Etchells, Duncan Grant, Cuthbert Hamilton, Wyndham Lewis and Edward Wadsworth.

In spite of Hulme's justifiable complaint, the English artists' "adaptations" of Byzantine art forms enabled them to familiarize themselves with the use of nonrepresentational design. Roger Fry spoke of the "incredible phenomenon" of Goncharova and Larionov's stage decor, pointing out that now artists could go to the "theatre to see experiments in the art of visual design—still more, experiments which indicate new possibilities in the art of picture-making."[30] The early abstract compositions of David Bomberg in particular were inspired by Diaghileff's ballets (figure 11). And a number of the works produced at the Omega Workshop, plans for which began immediately after the Second Post-Impressionist Exhibition, show the influence of Russian folk arts and crafts. This cooperative workshop, based on the principles of William Morris, was comparable to those developing in Russia at the time, with the important exception that the designs and crafts being revitalized were not primarily those indigenous to England—the paintings as well as the furniture, rugs and screens made at the Omega Workshop owed a great deal to the geometrical motifs and bold contrasting colors of Russian folk art and to the formal reduction of icon painting. As Fry had noted in an Omega Workshops brochure, "the artists who have associated themselves to found the Omega Workshops Ltd. are by nature predisposed to the study of pure design."[31] Of particular interest in this context are the highly geometrical rug designs by Etchells and Lewis (figures 12 and 13), executed while they were members of the Omega Workshop. These works anticipate the triangular shapes, stark color contrasts and decentralized compositional

Figure 11. David Bomberg, *The Russian Ballet Lithographs,*
1914–19
Four lithographs, from 5 × 6.5 cm. to 7.5 × 16 cm.
(Copyright Anthony d'Offay Gallery, London)

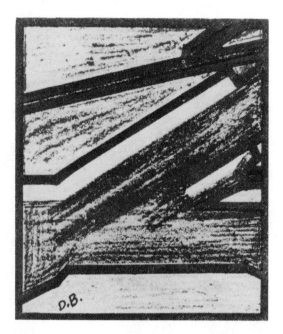

Figure 12. Frederick Etchells, *Design for a Rug*, 1913
Pencil, water and body color, 40.5 × 44.5 cm.
(By courtesy of the Board of Trustees of the Victoria
and Albert Museum)

Figure 13. Wyndham Lewis, *Design for a Rug*, 1913
Pencil and inks, 30.5 × 24 cm.
(By courtesy of the Board of Trustees of the Victoria
and Albert Museum)

elements of vorticist painting. When Lewis left the Omega Workshop, taking with him Etchells, Hamilton, Wadsworth, Roberts, and Gaudier-Brzeska, to form the vorticist group, the abstractionist vocabulary of these artists was already highly evolved. These connections explain in part the precociousness of the development of abstract art in England. For example, Wyndham Lewis's *Portrait of an Englishwoman* (1913) (figure 14), which was reproduced in Mayakovsky's magazine *Strelets* in 1915, is markedly similar to Malevich's later suprematist paintings (figure 15); and David Bomberg's *The Dancer* (1914) (figure 16) can be compared to Alexander Rodchenko's compass drawings of 1915 (figure 17). Examples such as these illustrate how similar influences can lead to morphologically comparable effects.

The adaptation of Russian neoprimitivist art in England has very different ideological implications from the same activity in Russia. In 1926 the Russian productivist artist, theoretician, and poet Boris Arvatov analyzed the implications of this resurgence of the arts and crafts movement within a capitalist society:

> While the technology of capitalist society is based on the most advanced techniques of mass production (industry, radio, transport, newspapers, scientific laboratories, etc.), bourgeois art has maintained, as a matter of principle, the production practices of crafts and thus has separated itself from collective social practices. This enables the artist to remain in isolation, in the realm of pure aesthetics. . . . The only type of artist in capitalist society is the individual, isolated master who refuses utilitarian production practices because these practices are based on machine technology. From here originates the illusion of art's purposelessness and autonomy, from here its whole bourgeois fetishistic nature. [32]

Arvatov's analysis applies for industrial England, but for postczarist Russia the development from neoprimitivism to abstract art to constructivist and productivist practices follows a very different trajectory.

In part, this can be explained by analyzing the intentionality of the Russian avant-garde's renewed interest in primitive and religious art— particularly orthodox icon painting. The banning of Goncharova's *The Evangelists* (figure 18) by the selection committee of the 1912 Donkey's Tail Exhibition on the grounds of sacrilege indicates the confusion that the adaptation of orthodox icon figures caused, even among members of an avant-garde group very much concerned with ancient Russian art. Certainly the greatest confusion of all was caused by Malevich's announcement that *Black Square* (1913–15) (figure 19) was "the icon of our times" [33] followed by his statements in *The Non-Objective World* that "art no longer cares to serve the state and religion. . . . It wants to have nothing further to do with the object as such and believes that it can exist in and for itself." [34] To come to terms with this apparent paradox, critics have been nearly unanimous in stressing the influence of the theosophically oriented philosopher Peter D. Ouspensky, particularly his metaphysical scientific speculations on the fourth dimension as the "Highest Intuition." [35]

Figure 14. Wyndham Lewis, *Portrait of an Englishwoman,* 1913
Pencil, ink and watercolor, 56 × 38 cm.
(Wadsworth Atheneum, Hartford, Conn. The Ella
Gallup Sumner and Mary Catlin Sumner Collection)

Figure 15. Kazimir Malevich, *Suprematist Composition (Supremus no. 50)*, 1914–15
Oil on canvas, 95.5 × 65 cm.
(Stedelijk Museum, Amsterdam)

Figure 16.   David Bomberg, *The Dancer,* 1914
(Copyright Anthony d'Offay Gallery, London)

Figure 17.   Alexander Rodchenko, compass drawing, 1915
Gouache

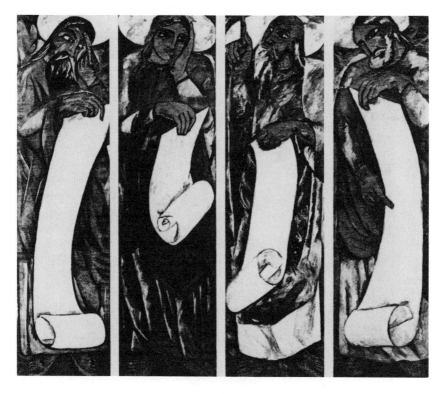

Figure 18. Natalya Goncharova, *The Evangelists,* 1910–11
Oil on canvas, 205 × 58 cm.
(Artist's collection, Paris)

Figure 19. Kazimir Malevich, *Black Square,* ca. 1913–15
Oil on canvas, 108 × 108 cm.
(Russian Museum, Leningrad)

What these efforts to explain Malevich's suprematist creation fail to take into consideration is the semiotic function of the ancient icon itself. The controversy between the iconoclasts and iconodules, of fundamental significance for orthodox Christianity, may, to a great extent, be seen as a controversy concerning precisely the semiotic character of the icon—the central point of which was the attitude toward the sign.[36] In spite of the icon's extremely formalized but nevertheless figurative form, it was originally understood to be nonrepresentational in that its "referent" was regarded as ineffable—the face of Christ could never be known. Malevich's *Black Square* lays bare the absent referent as the source of the nonreferentiality of the icon and calls into question the whole problem of any sign's relationship to the phenomenal world. In so doing Malevich exposes the idealism of the theological debate, the assumption of what Derrida calls the "transcendental signified," "which supposedly does not in itself, in its essence, refer back to any signifier but goes beyond the chain of signs, and itself no longer functions as a signifier." This allows for the metaphysical belief in a "reserve" or an origin of meaning that will always be anterior and exterior to the continuous productivity of signification. This tendency led to Derrida's assertion that a philosophy of language based in such a notion of the sign is "profoundly theological." "Sign and deity have the same place and same time of birth." "The epoch of the sign is essentially theological," Derrida observes.[37] Malevich conflates the signifier and signified. He does not, as is customarily the case, let the concept present itself in a supposedly unmediated manner, but rather he reverses the process, placing the signifier in the foreground and thereby circumventing the idealist supposition of the pre-existence of meaning.

This reading of the intentionality of *Black Square,* as an act of subversion on the symbolic order, is supported by a comment Malevich wrote on the reverse of *Cow and Violin* (1912–13) (figure 20): "The alogical collusion of two forms, the violin and the cow, illustrates the moment of struggle between logic, natural law, bourgeois meaning and prejudice."[38] When Malevich speaks of the primitive tendency in modern art, he does so in terms appropriate to his own use of the icon and makes it clear that the Russian adaptation of primitive art is not an atavistic activity, nor an act of cultural colonization, but rather what he calls a "decomposition": "It is the attempt to escape from the objective identity of the image to direct creation and to break away from idealism and pretense."[39] Primitivism, as it was to be employed by the avant-garde, was one of the major strategies to facilitate the creation of the autonomous, autotelic work of art—a work of art relieved of its semantic or representational function, precisely because meaning with an a priori existence had been repudiated; signification was now understood to be dependent upon the passage of signifiers themselves.

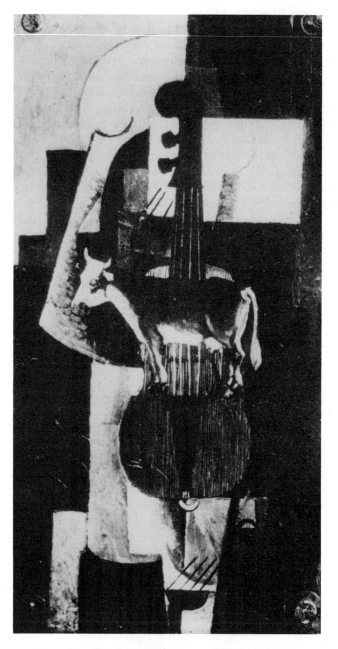

Figure 20.   Kazimir Malevich, *Cow and Violin*, 1912–13
Oil and wood, 48.7 × 25.7 cm.
(Russian Museum, Leningrad)

Connoisseurs of Chaos

The repudiation of the transcendental signified appears as the Promethean declaration of *Victory over the Sun* (1913), a theatrical collaboration by Kruchenykh who wrote the text, Malevich who designed the sets and costumes, Matyushin who wrote the music, and Khlebnikov who wrote the prologue. Malevich claimed suprematism originated while he was working on the sets for *Victory over the Sun*. A recently discovered sketch of the backdrop for the first act shows the square of the backdrop diagonally separated into one black and one white triangle (figure 21). The resulting two-dimensional effect breaches the convention of the illusionistic spatial depth of the stage. At this time, in 1913, Malevich wrote to Matyushin: "a different kind of reason has arisen within us . . . it also has its own law, construction and meaning, and only when we have cognized it will our works be founded on the truly new law of transrationalism." Later Malevich wrote to Matyushin that "this drawing will have great significance for painting. What has been done unconsciously is now yielding extraordinary results" (May 27, 1915).[40] Subsequent readings of this sketch by Rainer Crone and Charlotte Douglas suggest that the sketch may be seen as part of the sun against the dark universe, especially since the diagonal line is actually curved and may be the horizon line of the sun. They also point out that parts of the sun appear in the cover for the libretto (figure 22).[41] If this reading is valid, then *Black Square* may be read as the total obliteration of the sun, the climactic event of *Victory over the Sun*.

Victory over the Sun was performed in Saint Petersburg at the Luna Park Theatre along with Mayakovsky's play *Vladimir Mayakovsky, A Tragedy*, which also had a Promethean theme. Kolia Tomaskevsky, who acted in both productions, describes the stir caused by these performances:

Those who lived in St. Petersburg at that time will remember the picture of spectators arriving at the theatre. . . . There was a "sold out" sign over the box office. Numerous profiteers energetically bargained on the street in front of the Theatre and in the foyer. Scandal lovers from the St. Petersburg demimonde were willing to pay enormous amounts of money to get into the theatre. . . . Priest-critics appeared with stony faces: Yuri Believ of *New Time*, Kugel (Homus Novus) of *Theatre and Art*, [the leading St. Petersburg theatrical periodical], Izmailov of *Bourse News*, Rossovsky of the *St. Petersburg Page*, and others.

There were police—in excessive numbers—by the theatre entrance and in the foyer. Even the assistant to the chief of police, Galli, came. . . . His presence in the theatre indicated that the police were seriously worried about the Futurist performances.

There was so much interest and sympathy shown by half the audience and such a strong expression of revulsion from the other half that never in my entire life in St. Petersburg did I ever receive such a shock, or experience such a Cyclopean scandal during a premiere as I did then. There was a boisterous shouting at the top of their lungs from half the spectators: "Out! Down with the Futurists!" and from the other half: "Bravo! Don't disturb us! Down with the brawlers!" But even this tumult and scandal could not destroy the strong impression made by the opera. There was such inner strength in each word, the scenery and

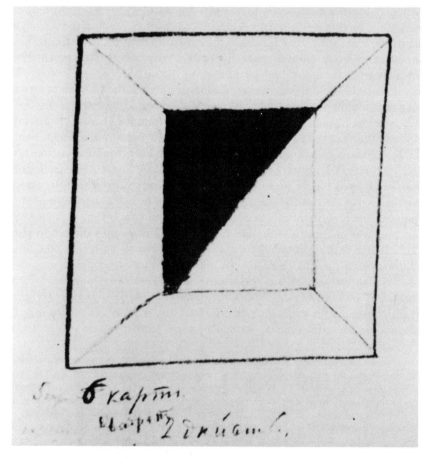

Figure 21.   Kazimir Malevich, backdrop for the opening of two acts
of *Victory over the Sun,* 1913
(State Theatrical Museum, Leningrad)

Figure 22.   Kazimir Malevich, cover for the libretto of *Victory over
the Sun*, 1913

> Future Man appeared so powerfully and threateningly in a way never seen anywhere
> before, the music moved so gently and resiliently around the words, the paintings and
> Future People and Strong Men conquered the cheap, pretentious sun and lit their own light
> inside themselves.[42]

Victory over the Sun is remarkably similar to Wyndham Lewis's play *Enemy of the Stars,* written less than a year later. Lewis may have learned of the play through Marinetti who, after having been feted in England in November 1913 by the then just forming vorticist group, went to Russia in January of 1914 just in time to be caught up in the furor created by the Russian futurist performances. The obvious similarity in the title, numerous small details in the play as well as the overall conception, suggest that Marinetti may have brought back a copy of the illustrated text of *Victory over the Sun,* published some time between the twentieth of December 1913 and the first of January 1914.

Marinetti approached the Russian futurists much as he had done the English vorticists: with, as Markov put it, "the pose of a general who had come to inspect one of his remote garrisons." The Russian futurists, however, were not about to be marshaled under Marinetti's futurist banner. Benedikt Livshits's memoirs provide a detailed description of Marinetti's stay in Saint Petersburg; particularly important is his account of a conversation which took place at a dinner held by the Russian futurists in Marinetti's honor. Livshits attempted to distinguish Russian futurist poetics from that of Marinetti. Markov recounts the events:

> Creation of neologisms seemed an insignificant accomplishment to Marinetti, who
> immediately reminded Livshits that the Italian futurists had, in addition to creating
> neologisms, destroyed syntax, used verbs in the infinitive only, and abolished adjectives and
> punctuation. To Livshits, however, all these accomplishments seemed superficial. "You
> wage a war against the individual parts of speech and never go beyond etymology," he said;
> and he added that a grammatical sentence is nothing but the outer form of logical
> statement, and that, despite all Italian innovations, the connections of the logical subject
> and predicate remained untouched. "One cannot destroy syntax in your way," Livshits
> asserted.[43]

When Nikolay Kulbin tried to explain the importance of the *zaum* or transrational language which Kruchenykh had just developed in *Victory over the Sun,* Marinetti responded, "But this is nothing but our *parole in libertà"* ("liberated words"). Then Livshits accused Marinetti of a "contradiction between what he wrote and the manner in which he recited it publicly, stating that during recitation he smuggled back into it what he had destroyed in its writing." Marinetti had just recited his *Zang Tumb Tumb* in which words were made to take on an onomatopoeic function. Marinetti claimed that declamatory aspects were only a temporary substitute in the process of the destruction of syntax. "We are more consistent than you," Livshits argued. "We abolished punctuation five years ago, but not in order to create another kind of punctuation to replace it; we wanted to emphasize that the verbal mass is uninterrupted, that its essence is cosmic." This assertion was too much for Marinetti, and he accused Livshits of preaching metaphysics (155). Marinetti was right; the Russian futurists were preaching metaphysics. What account Marinetti gave of all this when he returned to England a few months later is not collected in memoirs, but it is clear that the innovations of the Russian futurists would be a subject of considerable interest to the English vorticists. Lewis wrote *Enemy of the Stars* because, as he said, his "literary contemporaries were not keeping pace with the visual revolution."[44] He did not adopt Marinetti's theories and practices nor his typographic experiments but utilized instead a great many devices comparable to those employed by the Russian futurists. Mayakovsky's canvas cubes and "slightly slanted"[45] sets may have been the inspiration for Lewis's stage arrangements, in which "overturned cases and other impedimenta have been covered, throughout the arena, with old sail canvas." In the second scene the "audience looks down into the scene, as though it were a hut rolled half on its back, door upwards, characters giddily mounting in its opening."[46] A picture of the setting for *Victory over the Sun* shows an unmatched drop and wings hung upside down; in the sixth scene there is the unusual stage direction: The fat man "peeps inside the watch: the tower the sky the street are upside down—as in a mirror."[47] The colors of the setting in both *Victory over the Sun* and *Enemy of the Stars* are stark, unmodulated contrasts—predominately black and white. In the second scene of *Victory over the Sun* there is the addition of "Green walls and floor" for the set on which Malevich had written "green until the funeral"; in Lewis's play there are "the Red Walls of the Universe . . . till the execution is over" (*E,* 61).

The artificial light from the spotlights used in *Victory over the Sun* played an important part in creating the dramatic effect. Malevich had at his disposal a modern console-controlled lighting system which had just been installed in the Luna Park Theatre. Livshits describes how the "tentacles of the spotlights" cut up the bodies of the actors into geometric sections: the figures "broken up by the blades of light . . . alternately lose arms, legs, heads," presumably because of the absorption of similar colors by the colored spotlights. The blades of light that lit up what Livshits called "a night of creation for the world"[48] sound remarkably close to the bizarre, tremendously forceful and threatening lighting that pierces the night in *Enemy of the Stars.* "A white, crude volume of brutal light blazes over" the characters, crushing them. The stars, "machines of prey," shine "madly in the archaic blank wilderness of the universe." Iron throats drink the "heavy radiance, limbs [become] towers of blatant light" (*E,* 64).

The characters are grotesque abstractions of people, their bodies no more resistant to the powerful restructuring than the rest of the environment. "As with the metonymic fission of its acts and gestures, the body fragments into hosts of objects which can be foregrounded in their turn."[49] In Mayakovsky's play there is a man without an ear and one without a head; in *Victory over the Sun* the fat man complains that his head lags two steps behind his body, and a "Motley Eye" runs away watching the skull; in *Enemy of the Stars* a disembodied boot appears regularly to kick the protagonist, Arghol. Characters who are not parts of people wear masks and move like animations of monumental statues or distorted half-machine, half-human figures. In *Enemy of the Stars* the masks are "fitted with trumpets of antique theatre, with the effect of two children blowing at each other with tin trumpets" (*E*, 60). Hanp's was a "mask of discontent, anxious to explode"; Arghol's a "great mask venustic and veridic" (*E*, 59), a "head of black, eagerly carved, herculean Venus, of iron tribe, hyper barbarous and ascetic" (*E*, 67). Arghol "walks like wary shifting of bodies in distant equipoise." In one variation he is described as a "creature of two-dimensions, clumsily cut out in cardboard by coarse scissor-work,"[50] a description appropriate to Malevich's costumes which were made of cardboard and resembled armor. The actors in *Victory over the Sun* wore papier-mâché heads half again as tall as their bodies and performed with marionette gestures to accompany their "non-sense" words.[51] Matyushin noted that the Strong Men were made to seem gigantic: the shoulders of their costumes were at the height of the actors' mouths, and their huge cardboard heads towered above them.[52] Malevich's *Futurecountry Strong Man* (figure 23) could be the prototype for Lewis's *Enemy of the Stars* (figure 24). These are the central protagonists of the play.

The Futurecountry Strong Men and Lewis's Enemy (Arghol), are engaged in a Promethean struggle. Man against the sun is the paradigm of the poet's desire to overthrow the agency of meaning—the prohibitionary seat of representation, "the sun of cheap appearances" as Matyushin called it,[53] or "immense bleak electric advertisement at God," as Lewis put it (*E*, 66). "We pulled the sun out by its fresh roots / they were fatty permeated with arithmetic," the victors sing (*V*, 117). *Victory over the Sun* is a restructuring of an entire cosmology—language users, not space, time or causality, determine the order of the universe. "Lookers painted by an artist, will create a change in the look of nature," the prologue promises. Once the victory over the sun has been accomplished, the Elocutionist announces: "How extraordinary life is without a past...what a joy: liberated from the weight of the earth's gravitation we whimsically arranged our belongings as if a rich kingdom were moving" (*V*, 121).

The language and structure of both plays is closely akin to that of the carnival. As Julia Kristeva points out:

Carnivalesque structure is like the residue of a cosmogony that ignored substance, causality, or identity. . . . Figures germane to carnivalesque language, including repetition, "inconsequent" statements (which are nonetheless "connected" within an infinite context), and nonexclusive opposition, which function as empty sets or disjunctive additions, produce a more flagrant dialogism than any other discourse. Disputing the laws of language . . . the carnival challenges God, authority, and social law; insofar as it is dialogical, it is rebellious. . . .

The scene of the carnival . . . is . . . both stage and life, game and dream, discourse and spectacle. By the same token, it is proffered as the only space in which language escapes linearity (law) to live as drama in three dimensions. At a deeper level . . . *drama becomes located in language.*

On the omnified stage of carnival, language parodies and relativizes itself, repudiating its role in representation.[54]

It is exactly at this level—the drama located in language—that the two plays bifurcate. In *Victory over the Sun,* phonetic and semantic deformation and new meaning generated by them achieve what Jakobson describes as the "significant potential" of neologism, that is, its potential for abstraction.[55] *Victory over the Sun* is the creation of the nonobjective world. The old order of time, space, causality no longer obtains. Characters travel freely from the tenth to the thirty-fifth centuries of the future or "leave sideways into the 16th century in quotation marks" (*V,* 111). The final song of the play is pure transrational poetry—*zaum*:

luh luh luh
Kruuth   Krruh
Hee
Hoomtuh
Krruh duh tuh rruh
Krruh   vwubra
doo   doo
ra luh
Kuh   buh   ee
zhub
zeeda
deeda

This is the complete song, as meaningless in English (or rather transliterated, as here) as in Russian.

In Lewis's play, language remains incapable of detaching itself from representation. Even though at times the materiality of language is foregrounded and we are conscious only of what Lewis called "the finely sculptured surface of sheer words," these "sheer words" are not long at liberty—their referent soon overtakes them. Lewis's protagonist is posited in opposition to exactly the same forces as Kruchenykh's Futurecountry Strong Man. Lewis's play can be read as an allegorical enactment of Wilhelm

Figure 23. Kazimir Malevich, *Futurecountry Strong Man,* 1913
Costume sketch for *Victory over the Sun*

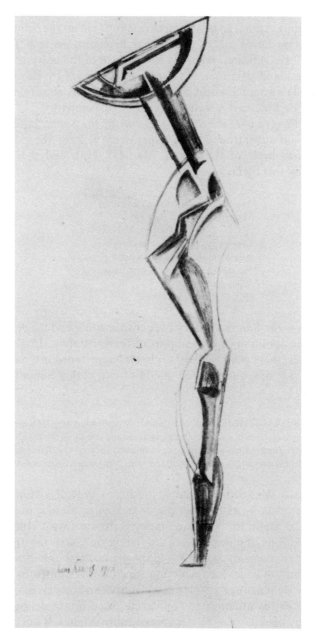

Figure 24.   Wyndham Lewis, *The Enemy of the Stars,* 1913
Ink and wash, 44 × 20 cm.
(Courtesy of the estate of Mrs. G. A. Wyndham Lewis)

Worringer's theory of two oppositional wills to art: abstraction (Arghol) and empathy (Hanp). Arghol is the abstract artist engaged in "the dehumanization of art,"[56] but as Lewis makes clear in the beginning he is a "foredoomed Prometheus." He is beaten regularly by the "will of the universe manifested with directness and persistence" (*E*, 66), and is beset by Hanp, to whom Arghol says, "You are the world, brother, with its family objections to me" (*E*, 73). Hanp is organic nature with its demands for empathy.

In both *Victory over the Sun* and *Enemy of the Stars*, "nature is not an origin, but a run-down trope."[57] In *Victory over the Sun*, "the violets groan / Under the firm heel" of the Strong Man (*V*, 115); and the poet is not constrained by this literary trope:

> The flower world doesn't exist anymore
> Sky cover yourself with rot
> . . . .
> Every birth of autumn days
> And blemished fruit of summer
> Not about these, the newest bard
> Will sing. . . .
> (*V*, 114)

In *Victory over the Sun* the victory over cosmic order and the destruction of nature are the abolition of conventions of representation. In *Enemy of the Stars*, however, there is no victory. Arghol is "imprisoned in a messed socket of existence" (*E*, 68), and his only mode of extricating himself is through language:

> Arghol's voice had no modulations of argument. Weak now, it handled words numbly, like a tired compositor. His body was quite strong again and vivacious. Words acted on it as rain on a plant. It got a stormy neat brilliance in this soft shower. One flame balanced giddily erect, while another larger one swerved and sang with speech coldy before it. (*E*, 66)

Arghol's decisive struggle takes place in the dream scene. It is within the dream whose characteristic is, as Kristeva points out, carnivalesque discourse, that language could attain its "'potential infinity' (to use David Hilbert's term), where prohibitions (representation, 'monologism') and the transgression (dream, body, dialogism) coexist."[58] In the dream Arghol fails to transgress the prohibitions, to enact the revolution which would transform him and his environment. He remains Arghol (fixed identity), and others recognize him as such in spite of his attempts to "obliterate or turn into deliberate refuse, accumulations of self" (*E*, 78). "He was simply Arghol. 'I am Arghol.' He repeated his name—like sinister word invented to launch a new Soap, in gigantic advertisement—toilet necessity, he, to scrub the soul" (*E*, 80). Nor is he able to rid himself of reality for long. He wakes up to find Hanp has followed him—"Always a deux!" In the end it is Hanp (the world) who kills Arghol, to the "Relief of grateful universe." "The night was suddenly absurdly peaceful" (*E*, 84). The execution is over, the universe satisfied.

Enemy of the Stars is Lewis's most daringly experimental approach to language, "a piece of writing worthy of the hand of the abstractist innovator."[59] "If anything extended could be done with it," Hugh Kenner observed, "this early style would be one of the most impressive inventions in the history of English literature."[60] At the same time, the dramatic action located in the language marks Lewis's retreat from the linguistic revolution. "Words and syntax," he decided, "were not susceptible of transformation into abstract terms, to which process the visual arts lent themselves quite readily."[61] This was the first step in Lewis's withdrawal from the abstractionist experiment. The second would come when he decided that "abstract terms" no longer seemed worth exploring in the visual arts either. The war that he had first complained had "stopped Art dead"[62] he later praised for having saved him from what he called the "abstractionist cul-de-sac."[63]

What Is to Be Done?

Many years later, when Lewis looked back on the period just after the *Blast* publication, he expressed a sense of missed opportunity, a recognition that there was some further potential, some next step to the aesthetic revolution which he had failed to actualize—which, in fact, he had failed to see: "I might have been at the head of social revolution, instead of merely being the prophet of a new fashion in art. Really all this organized disturbance was Art behaving as if it were Politics. But I swear I did not know it. It may in fact have been politics. I see that now. Indeed it must have been. But I was unaware of the fact."[64] There is a solipsistic strain in Lewis's excursion into abstractionism, as if he could only have dared to attempt such revolutionary work in a mood of boyish recklessness. Writing in 1954, Lewis described abstractionism as a "disease: the first case to be reported in these islands was mine, around 1913. You may imagine the sensation created—it was like the first Colorado beetle to be spotted in our rich brown fields, clinically free of odious sub-tropical pests."[65] But boys with bugs were out of place in postwar England where respectability, not rebellion, was the order. In an interview in the *New York Times* (May 1919), Christopher Nevinson justified the return of the vorticist group to traditional representational production modes by saying, "We artists are sick of destruction in art. We want construction." Even on the Continent, Nevinson pointed out, there was the same *rappel à l'ordre*: "So widespread is this tendency becoming that there is actually a classical reaction among the modern French. They are going back to Ingres." In another interview later in the same year, Nevinson's statement takes on a prescriptive tone. "The immediate need of the art of today," he announced, is for "a reactionary, to lead art back to the academic traditions of the Old Masters, and save contemporary art from abstraction."[66]

Given such a reactionary climate it is not surprising that Lewis recanted. However, in 1919, a beleaguered Lewis attempted to salvage his movement— this time without the help of Pound, who had left London because, as he complained, "there is no longer any intellectual *life* in England."[67] In *The Caliph's Design: Architects! Where Is Your Vortex?*, Lewis urged that abstract art be given a functional role in the life of the community. "What is the use of taking all the Gods away . . . and leaving the artist with no role in the social machine, except that of an entertainer, or a business man," he argued. "You must get Painting, Sculpture, and Design out of the studio and into life somehow or other if you are not going to see this new vitality desiccated in a pocket of inorganic experimentation."[68] Lewis's statements were prophetic: abstract art in England *was* desiccated. Nevertheless, vorticism was the first and remains the major abstractionist experiment in England.

Although the resurgence of representational art in postwar England obliterated the vorticist experiment, the avant-garde in Russia continued some of the vorticists' innovations. David Burliuk and Mayakovsky brought out a new journal in 1915 called *Took—A Futurist's Drum* (figure 25). Its dark paper cover, bearing the single word "Took" set in huge block letters of the sort usually used for posters, was clearly derived from the cover of *Blast* (figure 26). El Lissitzky, who was to develop typography into an art form in its own right, acknowledged the influence of *Blast*. "In England during the war, the Vortex Group published its work *Blast*, large and elementary in presentation, set almost exclusively in block letters; today this has become the feature of all modern international printed matter (figures 27 and 28)."[69] And, oddly enough, Pound's interview in Mayakovsky's magazine *The Archer* caused a revival of vorticist and imagist poetics in Russia. In 1919 a group of poets calling themselves Russian imaginists banded together to proclaim "The Victory of the image over the sense and the emancipation of the word from its content."[70] A more significant connection was the directive Lewis set out in *Caliph's Design* for the new functional role abstract art must take in order not to atrophy—to get out of the studio and into the street—and the constructivist theories that were being actualized in the Soviet Union at that moment. What Vladimir Tatlin called the "culture of materials" had pointed the way to a new proletarian art in which the artist had left the studio to take an active role as builder. "We do not need a dead mausoleum of art where dead works are worshipped, but a living factory of the human spirit—in the streets, in the tramways, in the factories, workshops and workers' homes," Mayakovsky announced at a meeting "for the wide working masses" in 1918.[71] Rodchenko repeated this in 1921: "Active work has to be done among the people for the people, and with the people; down with monasteries, institutions, studios, studies and islands!"[72]

The vision of the future and a sense of the potential of abstract art, so lacking amongst the vorticists, the Russian futurists possessed with an almost uncanny degree of clarity. (Khlebnikov in his first book, published in 1912, made a strangely accurate prediction about the collapse of "some empire" in 1917.)[73] They saw themselves as harbingers of a political revolution. According to Kazimir Malevich, "Cubism and Futurism were the revolutionary forms in art foreshadowing the revolution in political and economic life of 1917."[74] The overthrow of bourgeois taste, "smashing the old tables of aesthetic values" was the first step in "smashing the bourgeois order."[75] The subsequent evolution from Russian futurism to the constructivist practices of artists such as Rodchenko, Varvara Stepanova, Lyubov Popova, Tatlin and Lissitzky and their explicit politicization during the productivist period confirm their vision of themselves: their work is intricately bound into and supportive of the social revolution in the Soviet Union. "The events of 1917 in the social field were already brought about in our art in 1914 when 'material, volume, and construction' were laid as its basis," Tatlin announced.[76]

Art, which had traditionally used wealth, took on the role of producing goods—practical utilitarian goods that could be marketed successfully and used in the home, in the factories, on the farms, in the construction of buildings and of cities. "The artist is turning from an imitator into a constructor of the new world of objects," El Lissitzky wrote in his Proun manifesto of 1920. In this Promethean sense the artist-engineer, artist-constructor designs "Not world visions, but—world reality."

Figure 25. D. Burliuk, V. Mayakovsky, V. Khlebnikov and V.
Shklovsky, *Took—A Futurist's Drum,* 1915
Black lettering on dark grey woodchip paper

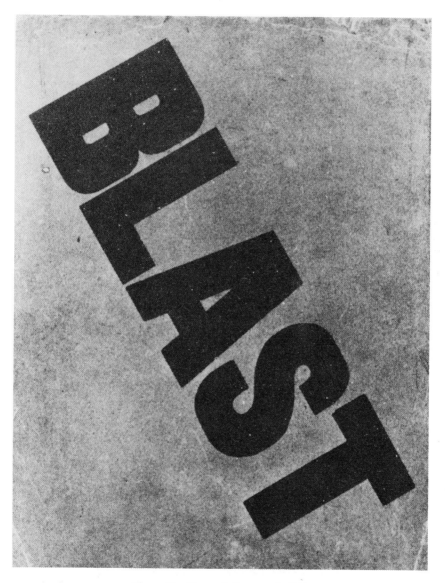

Figure 26. Cover of *Blast*, no. 1, 1914
Printed paper, 30.5 × 24 cm.

Figure 27. Manifesto from *Blast*, no. 1, 1914, pp. 22–23.
Printed paper, 30.5 × 24 cm.

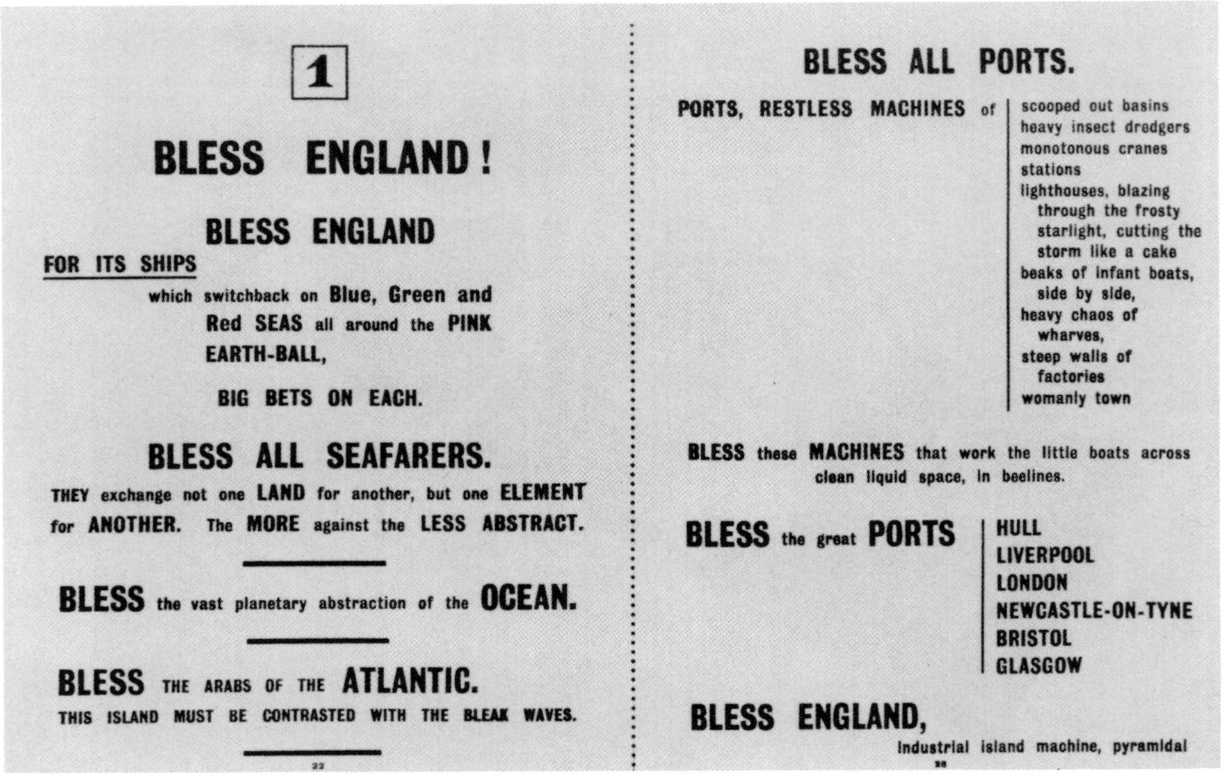

1

BLESS ENGLAND!

FOR ITS SHIPS

BLESS ENGLAND

which switchback on Blue, Green and Red SEAS all around the PINK EARTH-BALL,

BIG BETS ON EACH.

BLESS ALL SEAFARERS.

THEY exchange not one LAND for another, but one ELEMENT for ANOTHER. The MORE against the LESS ABSTRACT.

BLESS the vast planetary abstraction of the OCEAN.

BLESS THE ARABS OF THE ATLANTIC.

THIS ISLAND MUST BE CONTRASTED WITH THE BLEAK WAVES.

22

BLESS ALL PORTS.

PORTS, RESTLESS MACHINES of | scooped out basins
heavy insect dredgers
monotonous cranes
stations
lighthouses, blazing
through the frosty
starlight, cutting the
storm like a cake
beaks of infant boats,
side by side,
heavy chaos of
wharves,
steep walls of
factories
womanly town

BLESS these MACHINES that work the little boats across clean liquid space, in beelines.

BLESS the great PORTS | HULL
LIVERPOOL
LONDON
NEWCASTLE-ON-TYNE
BRISTOL
GLASGOW

BLESS ENGLAND,
Industrial island machine, pyramidal

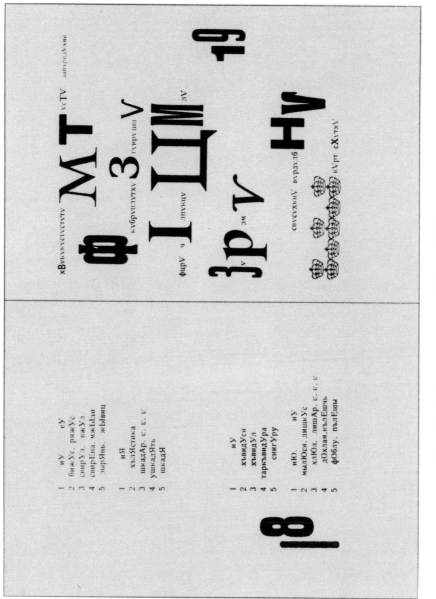

Figure 28. *Le-Dantyu as a Beacon*, 1923, pp. 18–19
Text and typography by Ilya Zdanevich; printed in Paris

4

Gertrude Stein: The Revolutionary Power of a Woman's Laughter

In the beginning was the gest he ⅂ jousstly says, for the end is with woman, flesh-without-word, while the man to be is in a worse case after than before since she on the supine satisfies the verb to him! Toughtough, tootoological. Thou the first person shingeller. Art, an imperfect subjunctive.

James Joyce

"When I use a word," Humpty Dumpty said, in rather a scornful tone, "it means exactly what I choose it to mean—neither more nor less."

"The question is," said Alice, "whether you *can* make words mean so many different things."

"The question is," said Humpty Dumpty, "which is to be master—that's all."

Lewis Carroll

For the most part Stein criticism has focused on Stein herself, not her work. There are more biographies of Stein than there are critical studies of her writing. This is indicative of the assumptions about her—that she was an interesting woman, led an interesting life and knew every interesting person at the time (one of her biographies is called *Everybody Who Was Anybody*). The assumption about her work is that it is boring, repetitious, childish nonsense. These are fairly accurate assessments. Her work is boring, repetitious and childish. Consequently, it is not well received. This is one publisher's response to *The Making of Americans*:

Dear Madam,

I am only one, only one, only one. Only one being, one at the same time. Not two, not three, only one. Only one life to live, only sixty minutes in one hour. Only one pair of eyes. Only one brain. Only one being. Being only one, having only one pair of eyes, having only one time, having only one life, I cannot read your M.S. three or four times. Not even one time. Only one look only one look is enough. hardly one copy would sell here. Hardly one. Hardly one.

Many thanks. I am returning the M.S. by registered post. Only one M.S. by one post.

Sincerely yours,

A.C. Fifield

Inasmuch as Stein pushes the signifying practice of writing beyond its limits she is subject to the accusations of producing boring, repetitious, childish nonsense. It is precisely in those issues and the inversion of conventional attitudes toward them that the revolutionary aspect of Stein's aesthetic inheres. "If something is boring after two minutes," John Cage suggests, "try it for four. If still boring, try it for eight, sixteen, thirty-two and so on. Eventually one discovers that it is not boring at all but very interesting."[1] As Kenneth Rexroth explains, the point is that the interest does not inhere in the item heard or read or seen, but in the repeated reception of it:

> Poetry is not the same as "please pass the butter" which is simple imperative. But Gertrude Stein showed ... that if you focus your attention on "Please pass the butter" and put it through enough permutations and combinations, it begins to take on a kind of glow, the splendor of which is called "aesthetic object." This is a trick of the manipulation of attention."[2]

This manipulation of attention or focus, termed "foregrounding" (the accepted English translation of the Czech word *aktualisace*), is defined by Jan Mukařovský as "the aesthetically intentional distortion of linguistic components."[3] Foregrounding depends upon a "background" of conventional devices, that is, language used in conventional and predictable ways so that it does not attract attention. Problems of intelligibility occur when the focus is not allowed to rest on the "background" of illusionistic literary conventions. "As soon as purely aesthetic elements predominate and the story of John and Mary grows elusive, most people feel out of their depth and are at a loss what to make of the scene, the book, or the painting. We have here a very simple optical problem," Ortega y Gasset observes:

> To see a thing we must adjust our visual apparatus in a certain way. If the adjustment is inadequate the thing is seen indistinctly or not at all. Take a garden seen through a window. Looking at the garden we adjust our eyes in such a way that the ray of vision travels through the pane without delay and rests on the shrubs and flowers. Since we are focusing on the garden and our ray of vision is directed toward it, we do not see the window but look clear through it. The purer the glass, the less we see it. But we can also deliberately disregard the garden and, withdrawing the ray of vision, detain it at the window. We then lose sight of the garden; what we still behold of it is a confused mass of color which appears pasted to the pane. Hence to see the garden and to see the windowpane are two incompatible operations which exclude one another because they require different adjustments.
> But not many people are capable of adjusting their perceptive apparatus to the pane and the transparency that is the work of art. Instead they look right through it and revel in the human reality with which the work deals. When they are invited to let go of this prey and to direct their attention to the work of art itself they will say that they cannot see such a thing, which indeed they cannot, because it is all artistic transparency and without substance.[4]

The optical metaphor is appropriate, for reading is first and foremost an exercise of vision. The child learns not to look *at* the printed words, but to look *through* them as if they were transparent or invisible. But Stein's opaque prose reverses this conditioning. It refuses to become a self-effacing medium; it will not permit the reader's gaze to pass, like light itself, straight through it. (A "surfeit of signifiers," Roland Barthes notes, "can keep the reader from enjoying a 'rich,' 'profound,' 'secret,' in short, a signifying world.")[5] Instead, the gaze is directed to the material object (or, more specifically, to the conditions of its visibility), thus effecting what might be called a reversal of figure and ground. The movements of semantic and narrative construction are suspended or reversed; the conventional ground, the transparent medium of language, which we normally take for granted, usurps the place of the solid narrative figure. Stein describes her method of composition as having been derived from an optical adjustment:

> The only thing that is different from one time to another is what is seen and what is seen depends upon how everybody is doing everything. This makes the thing we are looking at very different and this makes what those who describe it make of it, it makes composition, it confuses, it shows, it is, it looks, it likes it as it is, and this makes what is seen as it is seen. Nothing changes from generation to generation except the thing seen and that makes composition.[6]

Stein's intention, however, is not just to reduce language to its surfaces, but rather to conduct an epistemological investigation into the conditions of its visibility. Not only is the focus from figure to ground inverted, but figure and ground are also in a continual dialectical interchange. Each convention of signification Stein addresses she dismantles through an intensive scrutiny of what might be called the "pathology of written meaning,"[7] enabling the conventionally suppressed to come forward to the surface. She is exploring not subjective states of consciousness, but rather the structure of language that creates these states.[8] Thus, the reader experiences each dismantling as an expansion of consciousness, an exposure to one of the otherwise partially concealed powers of language.

The writing itself is the *instancing* of the continual discovery of ways to interrogate the generative nature and generative bounds of language, so that language itself shows the defining conditions of its constitution. This is not an attempt to master language by language, but rather to keep up a continual metalanguage athwart the text, to play a joke or make a pun that operates somewhat like the sentence, "This sentence has eight syllables." Stein provides a critique of her own practice in the only way available to her—in the guise of an amusement. The ontology of narrative art is not analyzable within the bounds of discursive language. It is not sayable in any serious possessive literal sense, but it can dis-*play* through its own playful lapsus its structural elements that cannot be eliminated, its inviolable conventional limits, its immanent possibilities. It may be, as Walter Benjamin suggests, "that there is no better start for thinking than laughter. And, in particular, convulsion of the diaphragm usually provides better opportunities for thought than convulsion of the soul."[9] In this passage there are echos of Rabelais's theory of laughter as misrule, disrupting the authority of church and state; of Freud's *Jokes and Their Relations to the Unconscious,* where the regalian power of language is disrupted by a witicism by which the whole of its domination is annihilated in an instant by the challenge of non-sense; and, in the reference to the body, an idea provocatively close to Barthes and Kristeva's notion of laughter as libidinal license, the *jouissance* of the polymorphic, orgasmic body. Benjamin suggests that laughter may be a revolutionary strategy:

> The class struggle, which is always present to a historian influenced by Marx, is a fight for the crude and the material things without which no refined and spiritual things could exist. Nevertheless, it is not in the form of the spoils which fall to the victor that the latter make their presence felt in the class struggle. They manifest themselves in this struggle as courage, humour, cunning, and fortitude.[10]

In asking for the response of laughter Stein is engaging in a difficult operation. The reader must want, at least briefly, to emancipate himself from "normal" representation; he must recognize that he shares the same repressions in order to laugh. What is revealed by this revolutionary laughter is the "fictive" props of the social structure. What is asked for is a sensuous solidarity. Could the resistance to Stein's writing be evidence of an obsession with meaning, of an unfitness for anything but a private, depoliticized *jouissance?*

Sense and Non-Sense

Stein's particular mode of foregrounding the materiality of language differs from that of her contemporaries, whose experiments lead to the creation of neologisms. From the accusation of writing nonsense, even in the neutral meaning of the word, Stein should be exonerated. She did not use words in an intentionally referential way to say something "about" a particular subject, but they always retained the lexical meaning they carried in the English language. In spite of the 1929 "Proclamation" of *transition* (the issue in which *Four Saints in Three Acts* was first published) that every author "HAS THE RIGHT TO USE WORDS OF HIS OWN FASHIONING AND TO DISREGARD EXISTING GRAMMATICAL AND SYNTACTICAL LAWS," Stein's experiments did not lead to the creation of neologisms or to anything comparable to *zaum* or transrational language. Her verbal revolution would erupt from within the English language: "She tried a bit inventing words but she soon gave that up. The english language was her medium and with the english language the task was to be achieved the problem solved. The use of fabricated words offended her, it was an escape into imitative emotionalism."[11] Freedom from meaning did not come easily for

Stein. "Of course you might say why not invent new names new languages," she writes in "Poetry and Grammar," as if to answer an imaginary interlocutor, "but that cannot be done. It takes a tremendous amount of inner necessity to invent even one word."[12]

Although Stein was interested in the presentational rather than the representational in language, she was not willing to take the short cut that neologisms provided. Conversely, her intensely immanent approach to language prevented her from attempting to break down the monological meaning system of language by overloading each signifier with multiple definitions as Joyce did. Joyce made the word elastic, both by abandoning at times its meaning, and by bringing out simultaneously *all* the meanings, dictionary or otherwise, it ever had in the English language or any other language. We will never find in Stein's writing a word such as Joyce's: babalbabadalgharaghtakamminarronnkonnbronntonnerronntuonnthunntrovar rhounawnskawntoohoordenenthurnuk! which can be "decoded" as an imitation of the sound of a thunderclap, composed of syllables of words meaning thunder from more than a dozen languages.[13] With patience, erudition and ingenuity Joyce can be understood. Stein claimed that Picasso once described Joyce as "an obscure writer all the world can understand."[14] For Stein this technique was merely a change of masters—Joyce was still bound by reference. Stein's writing derives its meaning from nothing external to the writing, but from her realization of what she presents in, rather than merely suggests by, her words. And that fact renders absurd any hermeneutic research into anything not presented in the words she writes down. "Miss Stein does not add to the already overwhelming dose of unassimilated facts and impressions which we all have to carry," the editors of *transition* announced, and they warned their readers not to attempt to "decode" her work as though it was a "species of modern Sanskrit." "Miss Stein has been reproached because she gave up adding to the great accumulation of human knowledge at an early age. Her greatness lies in this very fact. What is more salutory then to be able to read without 'knowing' any more?"[15]

Stein discovered, during her experiment with what she called "the recreation of the word," that once one elects to use words, it is not possible to make no sense at all:

> I took individual words and thought about them until I got their weight and volume complete and put them down next to another word and at this time I found out very soon that there is no such thing as putting them together without sense. I made innumerable efforts to make words write without sense and found it impossible. Any human being putting down words had to make sense of them.[16]

These were the circumscribing limits that Stein imposed upon her writing. Stein's experiments constitute an essentially "immanent" approach to language, an exploration "within" language of the properties and potentials of language, an activity distinct from, but necessarily concomitant to the use of language as a signifying system.

Stein's experiments with the signifying capacities of words, particularly in the 1911-14 style of *Tender Buttons,* "Susie Asado," "Preciosilla" and "Portrait of Mable Dodge at the Villa Curonia" which culminated in the lists of unrelated single words of *How to Write,* are similar to Tristan Tzara's techniques for writing a dadaist poem:

> TO MAKE A DADAIST POEM
> Take a newspaper.
> Take some scissors.
> Choose from this paper an article of the
> length you want to make your poem.
> Cut out the article.
> Next carefully cut out each of the words
> that makes up this article and put them all
> in a bag.
> Shake gently.
> Next take out each cutting one after the
> other.
> Copy conscientiously in the order in which
> they left the bag.
> The poem will resemble you.
> And there you are—an infinitely original
> author of charming sensibility, even though
> unappreciated by the vulgar herd.[17]

These experiments bring out the distinction between reference and compositional game, between an indexical system and a self-ordering system. Even in the random arrangement of words, we can impose meaning— grammatical structures will be formed by chance and, in our predilection for meaning, we are able to construct analogies with grammatically correct statements. Although Stein experimented with ungrammatical writing, meaning (the position of a subject of enunciation) and significance (possible, plausible or actual denotation) remains. But the semiotic process does not stop there. Instead of serving as the upper limits or goal of enunciation, the sentence or meaning or significance here acts as its lower limit or byproduct. "Indeed, however empty this discourse may seem," Lacan observes

> it is so only if taken at its face value: that which justifies the remark of Mallarmé's, in which he compares the common use of language to the exchange of a coin whose obverse and reverse no longer bear any but effaced figures, and which people pass from hand to hand "in silence." This metaphor is enough to remind us that speech, even when almost completely worn out, retains its value as a *tessera.*
>
> Even if it communicates nothing, the discourse represents the existence of communication; even if it denies the evidence, it affirms that speech constitutes truth; even if it is intended to deceive. The discourse speculates on faith in testimony."[18]

The conveyance of thought has, as Stein says, nothing to do with writing; "write" and "right" have nothing to do with one another:

> It is only in history government, propaganda that it is of any importance if anybody is right about anything. Science well they never are right about anything not right enough so that science cannot go on enjoying itself as if it is interesting, which it is. . . . Master-pieces have always known that being right would not be anything because if they were right then it would not be as they wrote but as they thought and in a real master-piece there is no thought, if there were thought then there would be that they are right and in a master-piece you cannot be right, if you could it would be what you thought not what you do write. Write and right.
> Of course they have nothing to do with one another.[19]

The Materiality of the Matrix

Stein subjected her writing to a technical analysis more normal to linguistic rather than artistic investigation. "Gertrude Stein," she says of herself in *The Autobiography of Alice B. Toklas,* "always had a passion for exactitude" and a "definite impulse then and always toward elemental abstraction" (73). She scrutinized the shape and sound of words, parsed sentences, investigated the structure of narrative codes, analyzed the nature and function of nouns, verbs, pronouns, conjunctions, and diagrammed the deep-structure (what she called "bottom nature") of characters as if they too were parts of speech. This desire to reduce every compositional component to its simplest paradigm is comparable to the way the early cubists followed Cézanne's injunction to "treat nature by the sphere, cone, and cylinder." Each stratum of her medium (the visible configurations of word-sounds, the semantic units and the representational narrative world itself) Stein brings to the surface, making each in turn disclose self-reflexively its *mode of giveness.*

Stein was most preoccupied with the first stratum—the sensuous materiality of words. It is on this level—the materiality of the medium itself—that Stein's explorations have most in common with those of cubist artists. The inclusion of words and letters in cubist painting marked an important step in the articulation of the materiality of the flat two-dimensional canvas. As Georges Braque observed, "They were forms which could not be distorted because, being quite flat, the letters existed outside space and their presence in the painting, by contrast, enabled one to distinguish between objects situated in space and those outside it."[20] Stein gives her own version of the appearance of typography on the canvas: "Picasso in his early cubist pictures used printed letters as did Juan Gris to force the painted surface to measure up to something rigid, and the rigid thing was the printed word."[21] Both Braque's and Stein's comments refer to the materiality of the letter form. When the two-dimensionality of the painted surface is articulated, the existence of the canvas as an object is pointed out; but the physicality of the picture plane is only suggested until the medium of collage explicitly demonstrates it by having the *surface support actual objects.* Always the viewer is moving in and out of two realms of perception—what he "knows" to be the case, i.e., canvas, frame, paint, and what he is led to believe he is seeing—three-dimensional objects in space. Collage destroys the picture as illusionistic representation and draws attention to the concrete materiality of the canvas.

There is an important correlation between the introduction of typography into painting and the decrease in representation of analytic cubism. Pierre Guiraud in his book *Semiology* notes that "the poorer the mode of representation, the greater the codification of the signs."[22] It is just at the moment when the conventions of pictorial representation were breaking down that the most highly codified sign system is introduced—language. The introduction of letters and words into painting asks that the viewer respond to an alien sign system—one that is wholly arbitrary, one in which meaning rests entirely on conventions of reception—and to make this response within the context of a sign system that is not considered to be arbitrary, that is thought to be able to provide visual counterparts to reality. In this way, the arrival of typography onto the canvas aligned the reading of the page and the painting. As if humorously to acknowledge the importance of this correlation for Stein, Picasso included a hand-painted version of the calling card of "Miss Gertrude Stein" in *The Architect's Table* (1912) (figure 29) and later used Stein's actual calling card in a collage entitled *Still Life with Calling Card* (1912) (figure 30).

In 1905 Picasso had made a series of woodcuts—single line drawings of birds—which were almost identical to the Egyptian hieroglyphics he was studying at the time (figures 31 and 32).

> The first thing I saw that showed this calligraphic quality in Picasso were several wood-cuts which he had made during the harlequin period, that first period of 1904. They were two birds made in a single stroke and colored with only one color. Besides these two small things I do not remember any other things of his which were really calligraphic until his last period of pure cubism, that is to say from 1912 to 1917.

Stein became extremely excited by what she understood to be the convergence of their respective art forms:

> In the Orient calligraphy and the art of painting and sculpture have always been very nearly related, they resemble each other, they complete each other. . . . It was natural that the cubism of 1913 to 1917 revealed the art of calligraphy to him [Picasso], the importance of calligraphy seen as Orientals see it and not as Europeans see it. . . . In China the letters were something in themselves.

This, according to Stein, Europeans never observed. "But for Picasso, a Spaniard, the art of writing, that is to say calligraphy, is an art."[23] Stein's own preoccupation with the "art" of writing made her acutely conscious of the look of a word or printed line on the page. At one point she announced, "I write entirely with my eyes. The words as seen by my eyes are the important words, and the ears and mouth do not count."[24] The possessive case apostrophe she refused to use because it spoiled the look of the word. Similarly, question marks, exclamation marks and quotation marks "are ugly, they spoil the line of writing or the printing. . . . "[25] For Stein these were shapes as well as symbols and should be judged accordingly. "The question mark is alright when it is all alone when it is used as a brand on cattle or when it could be used in decoration but connected with writing it is completely entirely uninteresting" (214).

Nevertheless, the semantic function is also a consideration in the inclusion or exclusion of words or punctuation marks. She liked periods as much for their looks as for what they do. But the comma, "well at the most a comma is a poor period that it lets you stop and take a breath but if you want to take a breath you ought to know yourself that you want to take a breath" (221). Similarly, Stein deemed whole parts of speech functionally redundant or uninteresting. For a time she avoided nouns: "Things once they are named the name does not go on doing anything to them so why write in nouns" (210). She judged conjunctions acceptable because they "work," and valued verbs and adverbs and prepositions because of their potential for ambiguity.

> It is wonderful the number of mistakes a verb can make and that is equally true of its adverb. Besides being able to be mistaken and to make mistakes verbs can change to look like themselves or to look like something else. They are, so to speak on the move. . . . Then comes the thing that can of all things be most mistaken and they are prepositions. Prepositions can live one long life being really being nothing but absolutely nothing but mistaken and that makes them irritating if you feel that way about mistakes but certainly something that you can be continuously using and everlasting enjoying. (211)

As for using words as pure sound, Stein herself gives an account of the infinite resource of this component of language—one she thought of at times as a temptation.

> I found that I was for a little while very much taken with the beauty of the sounds as they came from me as I made them. This is a thing that may be at any time a temptation. . . . The strict discipline that I had given myself, the absolute refusal of never using a word that was not an exact word all through the Tender Buttons and what I may call the early Spanish and Geography and Play period finally resulted in things like Susie Asado and Preciosilla etc. in an extraordinary melody of words and a melody of excitement in knowing that I had done this thing.[26]

Carl Van Vechten mentions in his preface to Stein's writings that there is reason to believe these two poems paint a portrait and make an attempt to recapture the rhythm of the same flamenco dancer:

Figure 29. Pablo Picasso, *The Architect's Table,* 1912
Oil on canvas, 72.5 × 59 cm.
(Collection of American Literature, The Beinecke Rare
Book and Manuscript Library, Yale University)

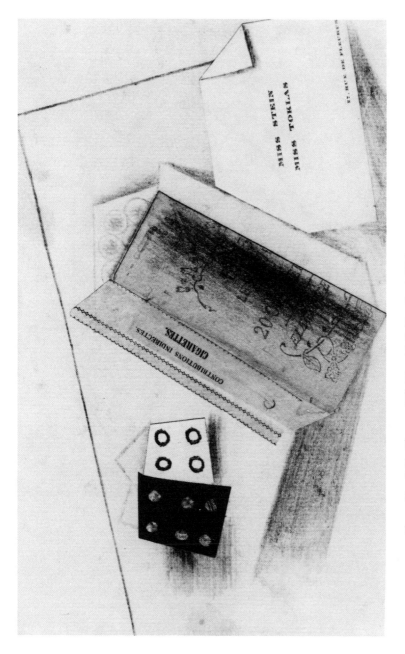

Figure 30.   Pablo Picasso, *Still Life with Calling Card*, 1914
Pencil and pasted papers, 14 × 22 cm.
(Collection of American Literature, The Beinecke Rare Book and Manuscript
Library, Yale University)

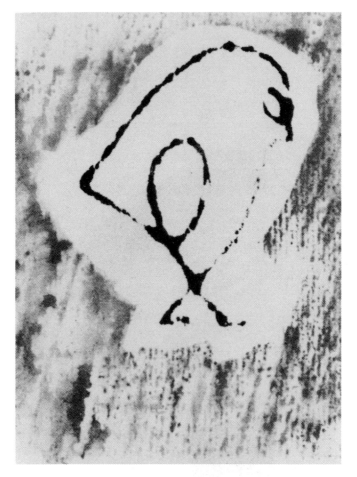

Figure 31. Pablo Picasso, *Composition bleue au pinson,* 1905
Wood engraving, 13.5 × 10.5 cm.
(Collection of Mr. and Mrs. John Hay Whitney, New
York; © S.P.A.D.E.M., Paris/V.A.G.A., New York,
1986)

Figure 32. Pablo Picasso, *Composition rouge au vautour,* 1905
Wood engraving, 14.5 × 11 cm.
(Private collection, New York; © S.P.A.D.E.M.,
Paris/V.A.G.A., New York, 1986)

SUSIE ASADO

Sweet sweet sweet sweet sweet tea.
   Susie Asado.
Sweet sweet sweet sweet sweet tea.
   Susie Asado.
Susie Asado which is a told tray sure.
A lean on the shoe this means slips slips her.
When the ancient light grey is clean it is yellow,
it is a silver seller.
This is a please this is a please there are the
saids to jelly. These are the wets these say the sets
to leave a crown to Incy.
   Incy is short for incubus.
A pot. A pot is a beginning of a rare bit of trees.
Trees tremble, the old vats are in bobbles, bobbles which
shade and shove and render clean, render clean must.
   Drink pups.
Drink pups drink pups lease a sash hold, see it
shine and a bobolink has pins. It shows a nail.
   What is a nail. A nail is unison.
Sweet sweet sweet sweet sweet tea.

If the poem is understood to be an attempt to limn the rhythms of flamenco dance, then the five emphatic beats with which the poem begins:

Sweét sweét sweét sweét sweét teâ.

may read as the stamping of the dancer's feet, punctuated by the click of the castanets and followed by the tripping rhythm:

Súsie ǁAšadó.

However, this poem is susceptible to various interpretations. Marjorie Perloff makes a case for the opening lines being the rapid, mincing movement of a Japanese geisha girl gliding back and forth gracefully as she serves tea; furthermore, she finds various semantic codes such as the Japanese sounding name "Susie Asado," "sweet tea," "slips her" (pun on "slippers") to support this reading.[27] Obviously rhythm is not being used referentially either. "Susie Asado" was the first Stein text that Virgil Thompson set to music. Thompson speaks of the freedom that the poem's lack of reference gave the composer: "With meanings already abstracted, or absent, or so multiplied that choice among them was impossible, there was no temptation toward tonal illustration, say, of birdie babbling by the brook or heavy hangs my heart."[28]

Repetition

In the sound of words, in rhythm and in repetition, Stein found a regenerative potential for language. The poem for which she is best known—the rose poem—came about as a result of her frustration with the flatness of overworked nouns. As she said, "a noun is a name of anything by definition that is what it is and a name of anything is not interesting because once you know its name the enjoyment of naming it is over and therefore in writing prose names that is nouns are completely uninteresting."[29] There are ways of releasing a noun from this fixity and making it new:

> But and that is a thing to be remembered you can love a name and if you love a name then saying that name any number of times only makes you love it more, more violently more persistently more tormentedly:
>
>> When I said.
>> A rose is a rose is a rose is a rose.
>> And then later made that into a ring I
>> made poetry and what did I do I caressed
>> completely caressed and addressed a noun.
>> (231)

Stein, in *The Autobiography of Alice B. Toklas* (137–38), mentions that Carl Van Vechten printed the rose poem in circular form in an early book (before 1914) and that Alice applied the poem to stationery, table napkins and plates. It is possible that Marcel Duchamp, whose name had been linked with Stein's in the scandal of the Armory Show of 1913 and who met Stein in that year, owes his famous female alias, Rrose Selavy ("Eros c'est la vie") to Stein's ubiquitous rose poem. Later, a contemporary artist, Carl Andre, exploited the plastic qualities of Stein's poem. "My plastic poem about the rose," Andre tells Hollis Frampton, will not be printed in a blooming, petalled pattern:

```
roseroseroseroserose
roseroseroseroserose
roseroseroseroserose
roseroseroseroserose
roseroseroseroserose
roseroseroseroserose
roseroseroseroserose
roseroseroseroserose
```

I have typed the alphabet in consecutive and contiguous squares. I think you have seen the result. Painterly areas of various and contrasting values are generated. Miss Stein wrote: "A rose is a rose, etc." and Miss Stein is not to be put down lightly. The word "rose" has a very different plastic appearance from the word "violet." The difference is, I think, worth exploiting.[30]

Andre, in priding himself on not shaping the poem into a representational rose, returns the poem to the traditional linearity of representational language. He did this perhaps to make more explicit the pun on "rose" and "eros," a point which he claims Stein obfuscates.

The repetition of a noun will eventually cause its phonic property to override its semantic function. At the point that the code becomes receptive to rhythm in opposition to meaning, language becomes invested with emotional significance. An important element of this cathected language is "the word perceived as word," a phenomenon in turn induced by the contest between rhythm and sign system. Stein fully understood the generative potential of repetition, particularly for writers writing in a "late" age:

Now listen. Can't you see that when the language was new—as it was with Chaucer and Homer—the poet could use the name of a thing and the thing was really there. He could say "O moon," "O sea," "O love," and the moon and the sea and love were really there. And can't you see that after hundreds of years had gone by and thousands of poems had been written, he could call on those words and find that they were just worn-out literary words. The excitingness of pure being had withdrawn from them; they were just rather stale literary words. . . .

Now listen! I'm no fool. I know that in daily life we don't go around saying " . . . is a . . . is a . . . is a . . . ." Yes, I'm no fool; but I think that in that line the rose is red for the first time in English poetry for a hundred years.[31]

This is Stein's refusal to sign the literary pact others have written for her, her refusal of what Barthes calls "this fatal character of the literary sign, which makes a writer unable to pen a word without taking a pose characteristic of an out-of-date, anarchic or imitative language. . . . "[32] Repetition is her way of fighting against those "ancestral and all-powerful signs which, from the depths of a past foreign to him [*sic*], impose Literature on him [*sic*] like some ritual, not like a reconciliation" (86).

Kandinsky in *Concerning the Spiritual in Art* (1912) touches on the potential of repetition which Stein would exploit:

The apt use of a word (in its poetical sense), its repetition, twice, three times, or even more frequently, according to the need of the poem, will not only tend to intensify the internal structure but also bring out unsuspected spiritual properties in the word itself. Further, frequent repetition of a word (a favorite game of children, forgotten in later life) deprives the word of its external reference. Similarly, the symbolic reference of a designated object tends to be forgotten and only the sound is retained. We hear this pure sound, unconsciously perhaps, in relation to the concrete or immaterial object. But in the latter case pure sound exercises a direct impression on the soul. The soul attains to an objectless vibration, even more complicated, I might say more transcendent, than the reverberations released by the sound of a bell, a stringed instrument, or a fallen board. In this direction lie great possibilities for the literature of the future.[33]

The Childish

This favorite game of children forgotten in later life recalls Kristeva's notion of the intonation, scansion, repetition and rhythm that precede the primary repression of desire in language. Perhaps, as Lacan suggests,

> we shall understand the celebrated maxim in which La Rochefoucauld tells us that "il y a des gens qui n'auraient jamais été amoureux, s'ils n'avaient jamais entendu parler de l'amour," not in the Romantic sense of an entirely imaginary "realization" of love, which would make of this remark a bitter objection on his part, but as an authentic recognition of what love owes to the symbol and of what speech entails of love.[34]

The best writers, Lacan claims, set their wits to postulating formulae that will satisfy the demands of the mysterious "genital love." This futile gesture he compares to the attempt to pull oneself up by one's own hair. For desire exists because there is language which is beyond consciousness and it is there that the psychoanalyst who has only a single medium—the patient's speech—tries to reconstitute the forms of love he calls pregenital. Lacan takes Freud's observation that the dream has the structure of a rebus, a form of writing, to say the unconscious is structured like a language; that is, the unconscious behaves precisely the same way as language and the unconscious, like language, emerges at the same point of primary repression. According to a number of psycholinguistic studies of child language, concrete linguistic operations precede the acquisition of language and organize preverbal semiotic space according to logical categories distinct from the functioning of symbolic operations that depend on language as a sign system. This is a very different view from that of immanent semiotics, which explores meaning that is thought to be always already there, and equally divergent from a Cartesian notion of language, which views thought as preconditioned by or even identical to natural factual data or else innate.

Studies of child language and certain kinds of speech disturbances such as aphasic regression render intelligible some of the peculiarities of Stein's style, in particular those characteristics most often pejoratively described as childish: the limited and simplistic vocabulary, the repetition of certain phrases or words which after a time take on different connotations because of the different contexts in which they occur, the manner in which these repeated words and phrases tend to dominate the entire passage, and the musical language—often rather singsong rhythms that result from this repetition. The aim of this aberrant style may be understood as Stein's attempt at reconstituting an early form of love.

Stein began what would be a lifelong investigation of language while she was a student in William James's psychology class at Radcliffe. With Leon Solomons, Stein wrote two articles on the results of experiments they conducted in an attempt to realize unconscious or automatic writing by diverting the subject in the process of writing. These were published as "Motor Automatism" in the *Psychological Review* (September 1896 and May 1898). The psychological aspect of language was what motivated Stein to begin her career as a creative writer. She began by listening to the "subtext" of everyday speech:

> I began to get enormously interested in hearing how everybody said the same thing over and over again until finally if you listened with great intensity you could hear it rise and fall and tell all that there was inside them, not so much by the actual words they said or the thoughts they had but the movement of their thoughts and words endlessly the same and endlessly different.[35]

In short, she is attending not to what people say, that is, their referential use of language, but to what she calls "the rhythm of anybody's personality." In "Melanctha" the characters repeat themselves over and over again in subtly differentiated versions of urban black speech:

> I don't see Melanctha why you should talk like you would kill yourself just because you're blue. I'd never kill myself Melanctha cause I was blue. I'd maybe kill somebody else but I'd never kill myself. If I ever killed myself Melanctha, it'd be by accident and if I ever killed myself by accident, Melanctha, I'd be awful sorry. And that certainly is the way you should feel it Melanctha, now you hear me, not just talking foolish like you always do. It certainly is only your way just always being foolish makes you all that trouble to come to you always now, Melanctha, and I certainly right well knows that.[36]

In an attempt to get at the "bottom nature" of her characters' language, Stein conducted an intensive analysis of what Freud specified as the two fundamental "processes" in the work of the unconscious: displacement and condensation. Roman Jakobson introduced these two processes into structural linguistics as the two axes of language—metaphor and metonymy, or selection and combination:

> The development of a discourse may take place along two different semantic lines: one topic may lead to another either through their similarity or their contiguity. The metaphorical way would be the more appropriate term for the first case and the metonymic for the second, since they find their most condensed expression in metaphor and metonymy respectively. In aphasia one or other of these two processes is blocked—an effect which makes the study of aphasia particularly illuminating.[37]

In normal speech both of these processes are operative; the speaker is continually making selections from the "filing cabinet of prefabricated representations" and combining these linguistic units into sentences according to the syntactic system of the language he is using. In aphasia one or the other of the two operations is impaired. The study of the effect of this blockage has established several laws of language acquisition because, according to Jakobson, aphasic regression shows the child's development in reverse.

In aphasics suffering from a similarity disorder, that is, those with problems in the selection and substitution of words, Jakobson notes that certain key words such as the subject of the sentence tend to be omitted or superseded by abstract anaphoric substitutes, while words with an inherent reference to the context, like pronouns and pronominal adverbs and words serving merely to construct the context, such as connectives and auxiliaries, are particularly prone to survive. It is difficult for aphasics suffering from this type of disorder to begin a conversation, but once the problem of beginning has been overcome, the flow of words tends to be of indefinite length— sentences are conceived as sequels to be supplied from antecedent sentences and the use of the same word over and over again causes a drastic reduction in vocabulary. Characteristics of the asphasic defect in the "capacity of naming" are apparent in Stein's early prose writing, for example in this segment of the portrait of Picasso:

> One whom some were certainly following was one who was completely charming. One whom some were certainly following was one who was charming. One whom some were following was one who was completely charming. One whom some were following was one who was certainly completely charming. Some were certainly following and were certain that the one they were then following was one working and was one bringing out of himself then something. Some were certainly following and were certain that the one they were then following was one bringing out of himself then something that was coming to be a heavy thing, a solid thing and a complete thing.[38]

Specific nouns are replaced by general ones such as "thing" or "it" because they are identifiable from the context and therefore appear superfluous to the patient, as they do to Stein:

> A noun is a name of anything, why after a thing is named write about it. . . . As I say a noun is a name of a thing, and therefore slowly if you feel what is inside the thing you do not call it by the name by which it is known. Everybody knows that by the way they do when they are in love and a writer should always have that intensity of emotion about whatever is the object about which he writes. And therefore and I say it again more and more one does not use nouns.[39]

Sign systems other than language depend in varying degress on the processes of combination and selection. Jakobson cites the example of the "manifestly metonymical orientation of cubism, where the object is transformed into a set of synecdoches; the surrealist painters responded with a patently metaphorical attitude" (92). Guillaume Apollinaire in *Les Peintres cubistes* (1913) noted the connection between the geometric relational units of cubism and grammar in writing:

> The new artists have been violently attacked for their preoccupation with geometry. Yet geometrical figures are the esssence of drawing. Geometry, the science of space, its dimensions and relations, has always determined the norms and rules of painting.
> The new painters do not propose, any more than did their predecessors, to be geometers. *But it may be said that geometry is to the plastic arts what grammar is to the art of the writer.*[40]

Stein's refusal to name the subject of her sentence, her avoidance of nouns and adjectives and her abnormally frequent use of pronouns, copulas, adverbs, conjunctions and other syncategorematic words (words that cannot be used by themselves as a term, but only in conjunction with other words: adverbs, prepositions or conjunctions; "all," "some" or "no"—which Jakobson describes as "purely grammatical relational units") may be understood as the verbal equivalent of the early cubists' preoccupation with geometry, a preoccupation they inherited from Cézanne.

> Everything I have done has been influenced by Flaubert and Cézanne and this gave me a new feeling about composition. Up to that time composition had consisted of a central idea to which everything else was an accompaniment and separate but was not an end in itself, and Cézanne conceived the idea that in composition one thing was as important as another.... That impressed me enormously and it impressed me so much that I began to write *Three Lives* under this influence and this idea of composition.[41]

The abolition of the central idea of a painting like the omission of key words in a sentence produces a decentralized composition:

> The composition was not a composition in which there was one man in the centre surrounded by a lot of other men but a composition that had neither a beginning nor an end, a composition of which the corner was as important as another corner, in fact the composition of cubism.[42]

Stein claimed that this same principle of composition—the inner balance of equivalent components—should also govern sentence production: "Sentences are contained within themselves and anything really contained within itself has no beginning or middle or ending."[43] More specifically, Stein's overuse of nonreferential, internally relational words can be linked to the dominant technique of analytic cubism called faceting—a modification of Cézanne's famous *passage* developed to reconcile the modalities of volume and plane. Those arbitrarily created facets or tiny overlapping planes were applied equally to the objects on the canvas as to the spaces between the objects (see figure 33, Picasso, *The Accordionist,* 1911). They did not serve to depict the object, but were purely relational in effect. Like Stein's overused syncategorematic language, faceting functions syntactically, not semantically.[44] Stein was fully conscious of the purpose of these nonmimetic relational units: "They were more important than anything else," she said. "They lived *by and in* themselves. He (Picasso) painted his picture not by means of his objects but by the lines."[45]

Once this contiguous mode of composition had been exploited to the point of near abstraction, Stein and the cubists began to work along the vertical or metaphorical axis of their discourse. Stein began to write what she called poetry:

> In *The Making of Americans*... I said I had gotten rid of nouns and adjectives as much as possible by the method of living in adverbs in verbs in pronouns, in adverbial clauses written or implied and in conjunctions.
> But and after I had gone as far as I could in those long sentences and paragraphs... I then began very short things I resolutely realized nouns and decided not to get around them but to meet them, *to handle in short to refuse them by using them* and in that way my real acquaintance with poetry was begun.[46]

And she goes on to make the following very deft distinction between prose and poetry:

> Prose is... the essential balance that is made inside something that combines the sentence and the paragraph.... Now if that is what prose is and that undoubtedly is what prose is you can see that prose is bound to be made up more of verbs adverbs prepositions prepositional clauses and conjunctions than nouns....
> But what is poetry....
> Poetry is I say essentially a vocabulary just as prose is essentially not.
> And what is the vocabulary of which poetry absolutely is. It is a vocabulary entirely based on the noun as prose is essentially and determinately and vigorously not based on the noun. (136)

In poetry, then, word selection is more important than in prose, where words are linked contextually. Jakobson makes the same distinction between poetry and prose:

> The principle of similarity underlies poetry; the metrical parallelism of lines or the phonic equivalence of rhyming words prompts the question of semantic similarity and contrast.... Prose, on the contrary, is forwarded essentially by contiguity. Thus, for poetry, metaphor and for prose, metonymy is the line of least resistance. (95–96)

Language forwarded essentially by metaphor or selection can, in extreme cases, result in the opposite type of aphasia—"contexture deficiency" or "contiguity disorder." The *combination* of linguistic units into a higher degree

Figure 33.   Pablo Picasso, *The Accordionist,* 1911
Oil on canvas, 128 × 88 cm.
(Solomon R. Guggenheim Museum, New York; photo:
Robert E. Mates)

of complexity causes difficulty, and the features of similarity disorders are reversed. "The syntactical rules organizing words into a higher unit are lost; this loss, called AGRAMMATISM, causes the degeneration of the sentence into a mere 'word heap'" (84). Word order becomes chaotic, words with a purely grammatical (i.e., connective) function like prepositions, conjunctions and pronouns disappear, but the subject tends to remain, and in extreme cases each sentence consists of a single "kernel subject word." This type of aphasia "tends to give rise to infantile one-sentence utterances and one-word sentences. Only a few longer, stereotyped 'ready made' sentences manage to survive" (86). This is a precise description of Stein's second mode of composition, which she called poetry. In her early prose writing, the chief stylistic interest is syntax, but in *Tender Buttons* the central concern is diction, the selection of words based on association:

> I began to discover the names of things, that is not discover the names but discover the things the things to see the things to look at and in so doing I had of course to name them not to give them new names but to see that I could find out how to know that they were by their names or by replacing their names. And how was I to do so. They had their names and naturally I called them by the names they had and in doing so having begun looking at them I called them by their names with passion and that made poetry, I did not mean it to make poetry but it did, it made Tender Buttons.[47]

And nouns returned with a vengeance:

> APPLE
> Apple plum, carpet steak, seed clam, colored wine, calm seen, cold cream, best shake, potato, potato and no no gold work with pet, a green seen is called bake and change sweet is bready, a little piece a little piece please.
>   A little piece please. Came again to the presupposed and ready eucalyptus tree, count out sherry and ripe plates and little corners of a kind of ham. This is use.[48]

The return of nouns, however, did not result in a return to referential language, in part because the nouns used are not descriptive of the object to which they ostensibly refer. This phase of Stein's writing, as in contexture-deficiency aphasia, tends to be characterized by what Jakobson calls "metaphorical mistakes": "To say what a thing is, is to say what a thing is like: . . . 'Spyglass' for 'microscope,' or 'fire' for 'gaslight' are typical examples of such quasi-metaphoric expressions" (72). Stein's "Apple" poem is intelligible (with some exceptions such as "carpet steak") as a series of quasi-metaphoric expressions relating to apples and various dishes made from apples. Stein describes the discovery of this mode of writing:

> I became more and more excited about how words which were the words that made whatever I looked at look like itself were not the words that had in them any quality of description. This excited me very much at that time.

And the thing that excited me so very much at that time and still does is that the word or words that make what I looked at be itself were always words that to me very exactly related themselves to that thing the thing at which I was looking, but as often as not had as I say nothing whatever to do with what any words do that described that thing.[49]

The relationship between the word and its referent becomes much more ambiguous in other passages of *Tender Buttons,* when the words are not made to combine with each other in normal syntactical structures:

CUPS

Cups crane in. They need a pet oyster, they need it so hoary and nearly choice. The best slam is utter. Nearly be freeze.
Why is a cup a stir and a believe. Why is it so seen.
A cup is readily shaded, it has in between no sense that is to say music, memory, musical memory.
Peanuts blame, a half sand is holey and nearly.

(182)

Sentences end with adverbs or just when a subordinate clause is introduced. As Stein pushes her writing along the metaphorical axis, the poems become mere "word heaps" with only "ready-made" or accidental syntax:

A NEW CUP AND SAUCER

Enthusiastically hurting a clouded yellow bud
and saucer, enthusiastically so is the bit in
the ribbon.

(165)

A CUTLET

A blind agitation is manly and uttermost.

(166)

Eventually Stein abandoned syntax altogether. In much of the writing that followed *Tender Buttons,* she did away with the conventional horizontal format of the sentence and made lists of words or phrases in vertical columns on the page.

Stein's statement about the arbitrary relationship between words and the object described is comparable to her statement on representation in painting—the interest does not inhere in the object depicted, but in the materiality of the work of art:

[A]ny oil painting whether it is intended to look like something and looks like it or whether it is intended to look like something and does not look like it it really makes no difference, the fact remains that for me it has achieved an existence in and for itself, it exists on as being an oil painting on a flat surface and it has its own life and like it or not there it is and I can look at it and it does hold my attention.[50]

More specifically, the structural premises governing Stein's second style of composition, or poetry, are comparable to those governing the second or synthetic phase of cubism. Juan Gris, who began painting only in 1911, in the later, synthetic phase of cubism, distinguishes between his mode of composition and Cézanne's. Like Stein, he sees the difference in compositional mode as analogous to that which distinguishes poetry and prose:

Cézanne turns a bottle into a cylinder, but I begin with a cylinder and create an individual of a special type: I make a bottle—a particular bottle—out of a cylinder. Cézanne tends towards architecture, I tend away from it. That is why I compose with abstractions (colors) and make my adjustments when these colors have assumed the form of objects. For example, I make a composition with a white and black and make adjustments when the white has become a paper and the black a shadow: what I mean is that I adjust the white so that it becomes a shadow.

This painting is to the other what poetry is to prose.[51]

Synthetic cubism and the discoveries precipitating the shift to synthetic cubism—*papier collé* and collage—are characterized by the disappearance of the relational or syntactical (what Gris calls architectural) device of faceting: objects are no longer assemblages of fragments, but are given their essential outline; color is reinstated, but not necessarily used to further the representation of an object; and *papier collé* and collage function polysemously on a number of levels simultaneously. They are colored, pictorial shapes that represent or suggest certain objects in the picture by analogies of color and texture or by the addition of keys or clues, and they exist as themselves; that is to say, one is always conscious of them as solid, tactile pieces of extraneous matter incorporated into the picture and emphasizing its material existence. Around 1913 to 1914 Picasso and Braque, as Edward Fry notes,

never tied their forms to a specific object, save when in collage a real object stood for itself and for the class of all similar objects. In the *papiers collés* and, later, in the fused signs of synthetic cubism, the forms chosen were invented, not copied from nature; and this product of intuitive invention differed fundamentally from the Cézannian composite form.[52]

In Braque's *Still Life with Guitar* (1912–15) (figure 34), for example, the two strips of paper have a purely pictorial function; they are broad, flat planes of color (blue and brown) that serve to establish the basic composition of the picture. The blue strip with the cut and hole serves to represent the central part

Figure 34.   Georges Braque, *Still Life with Guitar*, 1912–13
Papier collé, 58 × 49 cm.
(Arensberg Collection, Philadelphia Museum of Art)

of the guitar while the imitation wood-graining of the second strip mimetically depicts the wood from which the guitar is constructed. At the same time, they are fragments of paper attached to canvas. Thus, iconic elements reappear on the canvas of this period just as referential words returned in Stein's poetry, but in both cases the syntactical or semantic disruption precludes the referent from signifying in the mode customary to the medium.

During this phase of her writing, Stein relied heavily upon ready-made or previously combined familiar lexical units: copybook phrases, nursery rhymes, fragments of plays and various forms of phatic language: formulaic language that functions as filler rather than transmitting information, such as "How do you do?" and "Fine day, isn't it?" The same curiosity in exploring unorthodox technical procedures and the ability to see the aesthetic possibilities in the quotidian material of the verbal environment relate this aspect of Stein's writing to the collage and *papier collé* of cubism, which in turn can be seen as the precursors to the ready-mades of dada, and to the surrealists' *objets trouvés*. In Picasso's *Still Life with Violin and Fruit* (1913) (figure 35), *papiers collés* function alternately as ready-made and purely arbitrary signs. Fragments of newsprint from *Le Journal* are used to signify literally a newspaper on a table. Elsewhere on the canvas, newspaper fragments are given purely arbitrary significance, and at the bottom, a large piece of newsprint functions both as an abstract compositional element and as a sign for the tablecloth. In the upper right corner ready-made fruit—five illusionistic color reproductions of fruit—are incorporated into the composition by being placed in a bowl and transformed only insofar as they are assimilated into a new context. The ready-made aspect extends to the implications of the newspaper captions: "La vie sportive" and "[App]-ARITION."

Puns, collage, certain uses of *papier collé* and ready-mades function to convey meaning only in order to abolish it more completely. They are succinct referential denials of reference. Octavio Paz, in his analysis of Marcel Duchamp's ready-mades, equates the pun and the ready-made in terms of their gesture—the destruction of meaning and, what is the same thing, the idea of value:

> The Readymades are anonymous objects that the artist's gratuitous gesture, the mere fact of choosing them, converts into works of art. At the same time this gesture does away with the notion of art object. The essence of the act is contradiction, it is the plastic equivalent of the pun. As the latter destroys meaning, the former destroys the idea of value. The Readymades are not anti-art, like so many modern creations but rather *an-artistic*. Neither art nor anti-art, but something in between, indifferent, existing in a void.... It would be senseless to argue about their beauty or ugliness, firstly because they are beyond beauty and ugliness, and secondly because they are not creations but signs, questioning or negating the act of creation. The Readymade does not postulate a new value: it is a jibe at what we call valuable. It is criticism in action: a kick at the work of art ensconced on its pedestal of adjectives. [53]

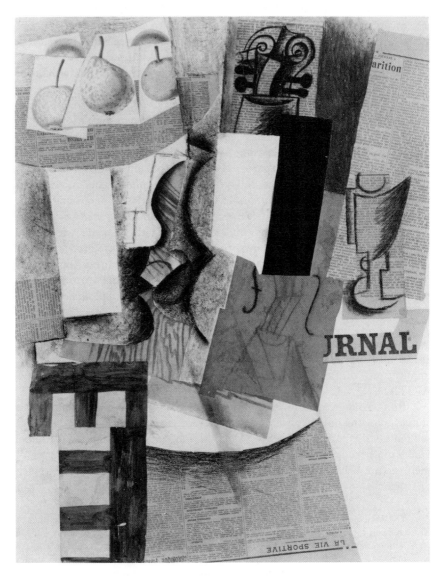

Figure 35.   Pablo Picasso, *Still Life with Violin and Fruit*, 1913
Papier collé, 65 × 50 cm.
(A. E. Gallatin Collection, Philadelphia Museum of Art)

The Pleasures of Merely Circulating

Puns produce another mode of textual irruption. By their semantic play they add a vertical dimension to the horizontal narrative progression:

> But, while the time-structure of the narrative is the product of an *irreversible, diachronic, cumulative synthesis,* the time-structure of the pun is the product of a synchronic, instantaneous unity; like metaphor, of which it is a species, the pun spawns a manifold, or polyphony, of meanings, simultaneously co-present. Being a cacophonous eruption on the linguistic surface, the singing of the pun inevitably disturbs the linear, unfolding temporality of the narrative progression. Together with pure sonorities and optical constructions, it produces nooks and crannies, bubbles, cracks, stains, and washes on the conventional plain surface of the linguistic canvas. . . . The good pun is not merely the dead trace, or pale shadow, of thought, but the living, self-moving motion of thought; it is language speaking by itself singing new meanings into beauty.[54]

Thus the pun, by calling attention to itself as language, causes a break in the production of meaning and brings into question the narratively depicted world, revealing the contingencies and lacunae in the depths of representation. It is the break in the text through which the reader experiences language invested with pleasure, where the orderly linguistic purpose is subverted and the reader partakes in the production of signification.

As Barthes points out in his analysis of narrative plots, the proairetic and hermeneutic codes—codes of action, codes of enigmas and answers—are irreversible: their interpretation is determined linearly, in sequence, in one direction. What motivates us as readers to pursue the meanderings of what E.M. Forster describes as that "dull, unlovely worm of time"—the story—is the desire to know what happens next. What motivates us to follow the unfolding of plot, based as it is on causality (the significant interconnection of events), is the expectation of meaning, the answer to the question that the plot posits. Ultimately, what motivates the reader is the expectation of the end, since for Barthes meaning (in the classical, readerly text) resides in full predication, completion of the codes of signification. Inquiries into the function of the end, as Frank Kermode has shown in his study of formal closure, have to do with the human end, with death. Or as Kristeva puts it, "As long as the son pursues meaning in a story or through narrative, even if it eludes him, as long as he persists in his search he narrates in the name of Death."[55] In a convergent argument, Walter Benjamin claims that all narration is obituary in that life acquires definable meaning only at, and through, death:

> The nature of the character in a novel cannot be presented any better than is done in this statement, which says that the meaning of his life is revealed in his death. But the reader of a novel actually does look for human beings from whom he derives the "meaning of life."

Therefore he must, no matter what, know in advance that he will share their figurative death—the end of the novel—but preferably their actual one. . . . *What draws the reader to the novel is the hope of warming his shivering life with a death he reads* about."[56]

Thus, the reader has quite literally become a *consumer* who feeds on the vitality offered by sacrificed characters. "Both the reading of novels and the analysis of character are acts of cannibalism at a metaphoric level; the ultimate aim of the activity is to suck the final marrow of meaning from the perfectly exposed innards of a perfectly executed figure."[57] It is just for this reason that Barthes rejects the realist epistemology in which the reader's role is that of consumer of the writer's product, and where both are motivated by a desire for the end. He favors instead the writerly text, in which the desire is not for the end but to put off the signified—the moment of closure, of ideological fixity—for as long as possible, to stay within process, the infinite play of meanings.

Stein makes the same choice. Her entire work can be seen as an attempt to circumvent the end, the closure implied in the capitulation to the "Law of the Father." "What is the use of being a little boy if you are to be a man what is the use," she whimsically asks. Once she extricated herself from any vestigial gestures of homage to a reality that has already been written for her, her writing becomes "a mode of Eros," or as one critic put it "a cubist *jeu.*" Her whimsical statements cover her shrewd awareness of the consequences of doing otherwise: "Writing is neither remembering nor forgetting neither beginning or ending. Being dead is not end it is being dead and being dead is something."[58] This aphorism is the *modus vivendi* of her writing and the rationale for her famous "continuous present"—for to circumvent closure it is also necessary to give up the idea of origin; the teleological assumptions of narrative are dismantled along with its ideological presuppositions. "In writing the thing that is the difficulty is the question of confusing time."[59] She was bothered always by the fact that in any narrative there is both a time in which the story takes place and another time in which the story is told—the difference between living and narrating:

I wrote a story as a story, that is the way I began, and slowly I realized this confusion, a real confusion, that in writing a story one had to be remembering. . . . It is this element of remembering that makes novels so soothing. But and that was the thing I was gradually finding out—realizing the existence of living beings actually existing did not have in it any element of remembering and so the time of existing was not the same as in the novels that were soothing.

And yet time and identity is what you tell about as you create only while you create they do not exist.

And so it is never necessary to say anything again as remembering but it is always said again because every time it is so it is so it is so. (181)

Without closure there is no meaning. In *The Making of Americans,* we are confronted with the interminable, with a modern Scheherazade for whom repetition is the stay of execution. The teleological assumptions of narrative are dismantled along with its ideological presuppositions—for to circumvent closure it is also necessary to give up the idea of origin. And the tale that is repeatedly told is the story of a text that writes about itself in the act of writing. The whole project is to repeat, "to go on now giving all of the description of how repeating comes to have meaning, how it forms itself, how one must distinguish the different meanings in repeating."[60] And the reader's role is to reread. "Those who fail to reread," as Barthes enigmatically puts it, "are obliged to read the same story everywhere... rereading is no longer consumption, but *play* (that play which is the return of the different)."[61] And as one rereads *The Making of Americans* one reads this story: "Once an angry man dragged his father along the ground through his own orchard. 'Stop!' cried the groaning old man at last, 'Stop! I did not drag my father beyond this tree.' "

"Every writer born," Barthes says, "opens within himself the trial of literature, but if he condemns it he always grants it a reprieve which literature turns to use in order to reconquer him."[62] But Stein never grants this putative father a reprieve. By the time one rereads *The Making of Americans* the Law of the Father is in a total shambles. "The tremendous cultural revolution implied by this interior revolution of technique tickles the very heart and liver of a man, makes him feel good," William Carlos Williams says of Stein's style. "Good, that is, if he isn't too damned tied to his favorite stupidities. That's why he laughs. His laugh is the first acknowledgement of liberation."[63] In this risible era of the New Right, libertarian laughter may be the only break, the only pleasure to be found in the plot being formulated for us. It may be that this revolutionary laughter is what really *enables* us to face anew—every year, every hour—what Hannah Arendt calls "the elementary problems of human living together."

Appendix

Synopsis of Interdisciplinary Art and Literature Studies

For those readers who are unfamiliar with the work that has already been done on the interdisciplinary study of art and literature and would like to continue their reading, I offer the following brief synopsis of some of the literature available on this subject. This list is intended as a personal sampling of my own course of reading. It does not include those studies in semiotics, structuralism and psychoanalysis that would inform any contemporary investigation of the relation between the arts, nor does it include works on individual artists or authors unless the works are specifically interdisciplinary in their approach.

Of the few interdisciplinary studies undertaken that explore the relationship between modern art and modern literature, most are in the field of French literature. In part this is because the most important vanguard movements, with the exception of futurism, have sprung up or have grown essentially on French soil and in part because the French literary critic could not help but be aware of the existence of cubist, surrealist, or dadaist writers. This is not the case with the majority of English literary scholars for whom the concept of a cubist writer, for example, is a novel, somewhat suspect notion. This remains the case in spite of the popularity of such writers as Gertrude Stein, William Carlos Williams, Wallace Stevens, Wyndham Lewis and E.E. Cummings, whose close links with the visual arts are very apparent.

Perhaps the best way to survey the scholarship that does exist in this field is to look at the two most common approaches: the *Zeitgeist* approach in which similarities between the visual and the literary artist are analyzed in terms of their shared milieu; and the other in which certain specific literary techniques are analyzed in terms of techniques employed in the visual arts. Naturally, all studies of this sort must examine to some degree the artist's milieu as well as his application of specific techniques to his own medium. Nevertheless, it is quite clear that certain scholars tend to one or the other approach.

Mario Praz's *Mnemosyne: The Parallel between Literature and the Visual Arts* is a kind of compendium or layman's guide to theories on the relationship between the arts beginning with the notion of *ut pictura poesis*. As a survey of the changing thought on the subject over the ages, it is an excellent guide. Praz's thesis, in which he describes the style of an era in metaphors of handwritings, is that:

> Each epoch has its peculiar handwriting or handwritings, which, if one could interpret them would reveal a character, even a physical appearance, as from the fragment of a fossil paleontologists can reconstruct the entire animal.... And what else is handwriting but the concentrated expression of the personality of an individual? Of all the sciences or pseudo-sciences which presume to interpret the character and destiny of man from signs, graphology is surely the one which has the soundest foundation. Handwriting is taught, and certain of its characteristics belong to the general style of the period, but the personality of the writer, if it is at all relevant, does not fail to pierce through. The same happens with art.[1]

But Praz does not, in fact, "reconstruct the entire animal." The vast historical span of his study precludes such a feat. What he does instead is to collect the fragments found by others. It is this pastiche quality that, in the final analysis, makes the work disappointing. The last chapter, the only one that deals with the modern period, is entitled "Spatial and Temporal Interpenetration." The title points to the central comparative issue in the modern period—the breakdown of the spatial and temporal distinctions between the arts. Praz does not really direct himself to the complexities of this issue; instead, he collects a number of provocative statements about various issues and presents them undigested to the reader. For example, when he deals with Gertrude Stein he simply assembles two pages of quotations from Donald Sutherland.

Helmut A. Hatzfeld's *Literature through Art* also spans a vast period of time (1100 to 1940) but limits itself to French literature. The restriction of the study to the literature and art of one nation has obvious advantages, not the least of which is the consideration of two art forms conditioned by the same social, economic and political factors and thus more likely to reveal a community of reflection. The theory underlying Hatzfeld's examination of literature and art is simply that a consideration, side by side, of different art forms within the same cultural epoch must increase the possibilities for interpretation. Placing a poem or novel beside a painting or piece of sculpture may very well reveal a new meaning of literary text, may illustrate the different expression of the same motif or theme "according to the separate domain and medium of poet and painter," may prove mutual influences and inspirations. However, as Hatzfeld stresses, the emphasis of this study is the "cultural pattern of the epoch." Hatzfeld's interest is particularly in the Middle Ages, the Renaissance and the baroque, and it is with these periods that his sympathies lie. He dismisses the cubists' and futurists' attempts to express dynamism by admonishing them with G.E. Lessing's strictures on the limitations of art. Apollinaire's *Calligrammes* are dismissed as an overstepping of "boundaries," an "aberration mitigated by a certain humor." Abstract art, with the exception of Constantin Brancusi's *Bird in Space,* is dismissed as "ugly—a shock to any kind of human or, to put it more carefully, Western or Greek taste" (197). He reserves his praise for artists such as Pierre Ray and Alain Fournier, who reintroduce a "dignified beauty at a time when art in general seems bound to indulge in discouraging problems and ruthlessly ugly forms" (210).

Unlike Praz and Hatzfeld, whose studies span centuries, Dickran Tashjian's *Skyscraper Primitives: Dada and the American Avant-Garde, 1910–1925* is highly circumscribed in time, location and intention. The limitations Tashjian imposes on his investigation enable him to broaden his scope in another direction. His study of dada in relation to American art takes shape, in its largest contours, as cultural history. However, even as he adopts the *Zeitgeist* approach he is aware of its traps and limitations:

> Within this frame of reference, art can be studied in order to understand the culture that produced it, just as knowledge of cultural values can illuminate a work of art. Yet I am wary of the first approach, and not simply because studies of that sort risk simplifying the art under consideration. Even if one treats a work of art in its complexity, exploring both form and content, an artifact that should at some point and in one sense be recognized as an end in itself is reduced to a means of understanding something else. Indeed, the reduction of art in such circumstances is always disturbing to me. Yet the autonomy of art also has its limitations. How much do we gain when we become aware of the cultural context of a particular work, and how often have we misunderstood a work because of our ignorance of its milieu and history?[2]

Tashjian goes on to argue that this is the only approach appropriate to the understanding of the dadaist movement:

> Because Dada does not conform to the model suggested by the concept of a movement, with all its underlying assumptions, a cultural analysis of the phenomenon is all the more essential. Within the realm of art history, movements are often assumed to be self-contained, unfolding one after another, as art comments on art. Dada, however, made a decisive break with art in an attempt to capture life itself. Consequently, viewing Dada artifacts solely as "art," irrespective of intent and context, would be restrictive. Likewise, though the central figures involved can be identified, the center of Dada shifts constantly from individual to individual. For a resolution of these problems, only the concept of cultures embraces a sufficiently broad range of human behavior commensurate with the diffuse nature of Dada, as it moved among the aesthetic, social, and psychological areas of human experience. Moreover, cultural analysis reveals the intrinsic incoherence of Dada by pointing up the essential tensions and contradictions of its structure. (xiii)

The chapters of most interest as comparative studies are the three that deal with the influence of dada on the poetry of William Carlos Williams, Hart Crane and E.E. Cummings. Tashjian does not attempt to label any one of these poets dadaists; he only tries to show the possible influence of dada on the development of their poetry.

Paradoxically, Williams was very vocal in his opposition to dada, yet Tashjian's study shows how much Williams had in common with dadaist notions. Tashjian speaks of Williams's defiance of accepted art forms and how the need for innovation led to the compositional techniques of *Kora in Hell*; of his interest in improvisation, simultaneity and the elements of chance; of his espousal of the spirit of change; of his desire to create poetry out of the insignificant or ugly—"the lifting to the imagination [of] those things which lie under the direct scrutiny of the senses, close to the nose"—and perhaps most importantly, of the way in which dada cut across the arts and facilitated discourse for someone who saw poetry in the context of the visual arts.

The case Tashjian makes for Hart Crane's involvement with dada is somewhat more equivocal than the one he makes for Williams. Crane repudiated dada's emphasis upon chance and was too involved with the perfection of his own craft to engage in "anti-art nonsense." He objected particularly to Walter Josephson's involvement with the techniques of the billboard. Where dada does influence Crane's development is in his critical attraction to technology. However, unlike some of the dadaists, Crane did not want to embrace the machine directly; rather he wanted to bring the machine within the ambience of art. Although Crane learned techniques for the incorporation of technology into art from the dadaists, he was, in doing so, following the tradition of Walt Whitman, not Duchamp. Crane acknowledged Whitman for being "able to coordinate those forces in America which seem most intractable, fusing them into a universal vision which takes on additional significance as time goes on."[3]

In the chapter on E.E. Cummings, Tashjian shows how Cummings, in his willingness to experiment with typography and in his daring to play with various poetic techniques, held easy discourse with the avant-garde art movement. Tashjian not only outlines shared aesthetic preoccupations, but he presents a close analysis of the specific avant-garde activities that influenced Cummings. For example, Cummings would have been in accord with the De Stijl manifesto of 1920, proclaimed by Theo van Doesburg, who had been inspired by the literary experiments of dada. After asserting that "the verb is Dead," van Doesburg presents a full-scale plan for rejuvenating language. Cummings would have read this manifesto when it reappeared in the spring 1925 issue of *The Little Review*. As he noted in the foreword to the 1926 publication of *Is 5*, the manifesto was the beginning of his "Ineluctable preoccupation with the Verb." Further, Tashjian shows how the verbal experimentation of Richard Huelsenbeck, particularly his abstract poetry which was published in *The Little Review,* influenced Cummings's experimentations. Tashjian also shows how the dadaist exploration of the possibilities of simultaneity was a stepping-stone for Cummings's much more sophisticated innovations in simultaneity: the breakdown of a sequential sense of time, suggesting "that actual Present" as he phrased it in *The Enormous Room.*[4]

Perhaps the best known comparative study is Wylie Sypher's *Rococo to Cubism in Art and Literature.* Sypher relies primarily on the *Zeitgeist* approach. He explains the assumptions upon which his study is based by quoting Pierre Francastel's *Peinture et société:* "Technique alone is powerless to account for the appearance of a new style, for a new style in art means the appearance of a new attitude of man to the world."[5] The *Zeitgeist* of any era is revealed, according to Sypher, through style: "A style is a vocabulary. It may well be the most sensitive and explicit vocabulary of any society. If style is a vocabulary, it is also a syntax, and syntax expresses the way in which a society feels, responds, thinks, communicates, dreads, escapes...." (307). It is Sypher's attempt to trace, through the tricky and problematic principle of style, the translucent and pervading forms of thought developing through each era that makes his work so impressive. Herein also lie its limitations, for the subject of the book is so vast and vague that the reader is forced to rely on Sypher's intuitive grasp of the general mental attitude of a particular era; and the nature of the subject perhaps accounts for the language in which the book is written. Sypher expresses most of his ideas in terms of metaphors, and these metaphors, while vivid and forceful, frequently usurp the ideas they are trying to convey. Sypher's work is important because it is a seminal study and subsequent attempts at this kind of comparative study cannot help but be indebted to him. However, because Sypher provides so little in the way of a methodology for comparing the arts, so few principles or guidelines by which these kinds of comparison may legitimately be carried out, those not gifted with Sypher's facility with language are left with little to go on. A further drawback to Sypher's work for those interested in English literature, is that the modern section, except for a few erroneous observations about T.S. Eliot, omits English writers altogether.

Unlike Sypher, whose language and imagination constantly delight if they do not always inform, Georges Lemaître in his book *From Cubism to Surrealism in French Literature* manages to make the most interesting, revolutionary ideas and people appear pompous and dull. His might be classified as the *Zeitgeist* approach mainly in default of any close analysis of individual works. He does give a lengthy account of the various art movements before going on to discuss individual writers, but the relationship between the two is only rarely touched upon and then either the most obvious parallels are pointed out or pseudoparallels are made such as the one in the following rhetorical flourish:

When the poet reaches this ecstatic stage, [one Lemaître claims Apollinaire has reached], he rises well above all human limitations. Like the Cubist painter, the Cubist poet brings us the revelation of another world, seen through the intuitive power of the mind and lying beyond the reach of the "normal" man. A few normal men may perhaps be initiated indirectly and may eventually catch a reflection of the "vision splendid" that illuminates the spirit of an Apollinaire. To the majority, however, this vision will always remain inaccessible. Like the prophets of old, the modern poet will encounter incredulity and contempt. Yet he will remain confident in his mission, because he knows that he proclaims a world that is super-human and though challenging belief, supremely real and true.[6]

Such a diffuse, almost impressionistic style is what mars the more substantial scholarship of Marcel Raymond's *From Baudelaire to Surrealism*. It is not Raymond's intention to show the influence of the visual arts on modern French poetry. In fact, at one point Raymond suggests that such comparisons are invalid. He says of cubist poetry:

The essence of this poetry which has often been called cubist—to mark its affinity with the painting of Picasso—is that it is protean and virtually inaccessible. The best thing is to bring to light a few elements of these pseudo-cubists and to trace one or two of the routes that they have opened to the effervescent activity of a new generation.[7]

The inference is that only the most tenuous connection exists between the painting of Picasso and that poetry that Lemaître characterizes as "protean and virtually inaccessible." Nevertheless, there are in this study a number of cogent observations regarding the close and mutually beneficial relationship that existed between the arts in the early part of the twentieth century. Among the most important aspects Raymond discusses are the following: the rejection of the romanticism of the impressionists and the attempt to accept the rhythms of the machine civilization; the liberation from the obligation to imitate anything or to mean anything; and the acceptance of the banal and the ugly. These aspects of modern French poetry, Raymond asserts, have developed because the cubist painters have given valuable aid to the poet.

Gerald Kamber's work *Max Jacob and the Poetics of Cubism* is an extreme example of the second major approach—that of closely comparing a particular piece of literature with a particular painting. Kamber's close analysis of particular works is at first refreshing after the rather diffuse discussions mentioned earlier, but it shortly becomes very pedantic. For example, Kamber devotes ten pages to a close analysis of Juan Gris's *Violon et danier* and Max Jacob's *Equatoriales solitaires*. Every item in the picture is analyzed, and in the poem every image, every pun, every sound (complete with its phonetic symbol and whether it is a glottal stop or a fricative) is analyzed with painstaking care. After all this, the only reason given for discussing these two works together, is that "there is in the picture and poem the same fine disregard for the conventions of rationality and logic, the same lack of transitions, the same fragmentation."[8] This observation could be made about any number of poems and paintings and could easily be made about these two particular works without the lengthy, close analysis. On another occasion Kamber lists all the poems by Max Jacob that have the word "cubism" in them. The commentary that follows each of these poems ranges from an explanation of the puns to interpreting certain images in terms of biographical incidents. Never is mention made of anything to do with cubism—the ostensible reason for this collection of poems.

What Kamber's study lacks, primarily, is any coherent methodology for comparing the two arts. In its attempt to formulate a methodology, Bram Dijkstra's *The Hieroglyphics of a New Speech: Cubism, Stieglitz and the Early Poetry of William Carlos Williams* is of interest not just to devotees of Williams, but to those interested in solutions to the problems posed by such comparisons. He begins by giving an account of the New York avant-garde in the early 1900s. This is not a "tracing of a drama on the spiritual plane" in order to reveal a "mysterious coherence"; it is a well-documented account of the Armory Show of 1913, the people and activities surrounding Alfred Stieglitz and his studio "291," and the publication of *Camera Work, 291,* and *The Little Review.* What this first chapter reveals is how closely painters, writers and photographers of this very active group were working together to formulate a coherent modern American aesthetic. In the second chapter Dijkstra traces the ways in which cubist theories and techniques shaped the early evolution of Williams's poetry and poetics. He shows for example, how Williams's treatment of the poetic image, the space that surrounds an image, and the multiple random relationships of the various images in a poem were derived from specific paintings. Dijkstra's careful illustration of the ways in which certain visual techniques may be translated into the verbal medium, though brief (they are limited to one short chapter) and focused on Williams's poetry only, are a step toward formulating the basis by which comparative studies may be carried out.

Beginning with Wylie Sypher, almost every critic who has written on Gertrude Stein, even briefly, has attempted to take into account the influence that the artists who surrounded her exerted on her writing.[9] Michael Hoffman's *The Development of Abstractionism in the Writings of Gertrude Stein* was the first systematic exploration of the formal relationships between Stein's writing and analytic and synthetic cubism. His book, written in 1965, has informed all subsequent investigations of the comparison, including my own. A recent study by Randa Kay Dubnick, *The Structure of Obscurity: Gertrude Stein, Language, and Cubism,* makes excellent use of studies in structural linguistics in its comparison of the mode of production of visual and verbal sign systems. A section of the preceding chapter of the present work, on Stein, is indebted to Dubnick, and I would recommend her much more detailed analysis to the reader interested in this aspect of Stein's writing.

Another excellent study is Wendy Steiner's *Exact Resemblance to Exact Resemblance: The Literary Portraiture of Gertrude Stein*. Literary portraiture seems like a conservative genre to be examining in the context of so faithful an adherent of modernism as Stein; however, Steiner's examination shows how the literary portrait, with its conceptual dependence upon its counterpart in the graphic arts, makes the modernist issue of self-reflexiveness versus reference stand out in high relief. The chapter devoted to literary cubism is rewarding in its close comparative analysis, but Steiner uses the difference in semiotic function between writing and painting (i.e., words are signs while paint need not be) as the grounds for claiming that Stein's most fully experimental writing failed. My own contention is that Stein was one of the first writers to explore fully the differences in semiotic functions for a very strategic insurrection of the semiotic process itself.

Wendy Steiner has written another fine work on the issues raised by the study of interartistic relationships, *The Colors of Rhetoric: Problems in the Relation between Modern Literature and Painting*. The first chapter of the book is a comprehensive historical account of this discussion beginning with Simonides and ending with modern poets, painters and theoreticians. The book manages to combine the disparate disciplines of art history, literary scholarship, linguistics and semiotics with a close analysis of modern poetry and painting. Particularly rewarding is Steiner's chapter on concrete poetry.

There are, besides these comparative works, studies of a more historical nature that at times engage in exploring the relationship between the arts. The research contained in these works provides a great deal of the necessary data upon which comparative studies must draw.

LeRoy C. Breunig's *Guillaume Apollinaire* is a general study of Apollinaire's poetry and criticism. Naturally some comparative investigation is inevitable in dealing with a writer who campaigned so hard for a collaboration between the arts. When Breunig addresses the subject of Apollinaire's poetic innovations and their relationship to the pictorial innovations of his associates, he does so in such an intelligent fashion that the book becomes worth reading not just for those interested in Apollinaire, but for those interested in the development of modern literature in general. The parallels Breunig draws between the arts are never forced. He is careful to point out where Apollinaire's "Zone," which is usually cited as the great cubist poem, fails to overcome its basic sequential nature in spite of a proliferation of verbal techniques developed to convey the sense of simultaneity. On the other hand, Breunig is able to illustrate the more genuinely cubistic qualities of such hitherto neglected poems as "Les Fiançailles" and "Le Voyageur." It is unfortunate that Breunig's study is so brief.

Marianne Martin's excellent history of futurism, *Futurist Art and Theory,* is important for the way it reveals the very considerable literary aspect of futurism. Although she focuses mainly on the painters, Martin does discuss throughout the book the activities of the numerous futurist poets: Libero Altomane, Paolo Buzzi, Luciano Folgore, Felix Fénéon, Aldo Palazzeschi, Italo Tovolato, Luigi Russolo (who was a member of the *Poesia* circle before he turned to painting and then to music), Umberto Boccioni (whose early literary activities helped formulate aesthetic theories that would come to fruition in his paintings), Ardengo Soffici (who also began his artistic career as a writer) and, of course, Marinetti himself. Martin's careful detailing of the early stages of futurism is a reminder that futurism was originally a literary movement. She traces the development of futurist aesthetic theories through such literary reviews as *Leonardo, La Voce, Lacerba* and *Poesia.* She points out that the first futurist manifesto was a prose-poem written by Marinetti, who had a considerable literary reputation by this time. The first manifesto was primarily literary in reference; it was not until a year later that nonliterary artists joined the movement. There followed two other literary manifestos: The *Dramatist Manifesto* and the *Technical Manifesto of Literature* which was written in a clipped, unadorned, telegraphic style. This was a more radical statement of *parole in libertà.* It extended the typographical and onomatopoeic elements of Marinetti's earlier work, suggested the use of three or four colors of ink and twenty different typefaces, advocated the deforming and remodeling of words by cutting or lengthening them. In short, most of the suggestions openly invaded the domain of the visual arts.

The same overlapping is true of Christopher Green's book *Léger and the Avant-Garde.* Green intends to provide an analysis of the formative influences on Fernand Léger, and in doing so he includes a discussion of the joint efforts of poets and painters of the Parisian avant-garde to formulate a "collective aesthetic" that would reflect "present day life, more fragmented, faster than that of previous epochs."[10] For the most part, the parallels Green draws between the arts are thematic ones. He discusses the theory called unanimism—"The belief that by feeling people can so identify with each other and with their surroundings that they can lose their isolation, become one" (22). This belief in the interpenetration of people and things, shared by the Abbaye de Créteil writers, Green relates to the effects of interpenetration in the paintings of Albert Gleizes, Jean Metzinger, Duchamp, and Léger. The interpenetration theme explains, in part, the importance of the subject of the city. "For the poets as much as the painters, the city was perhaps the most powerful symbol of the rhythmic interpenetration of living things, and of *la durée*" (28). The subject of the city was expressed in such poems as Emile Verhaeren's *Villes tentaculaires,* Jules Romains's *La Vie unanime* and *Un Etre en marche,* as well as paintings such as Delaunay's *Tours* and Léger's *Les Fumées sur les toits.* The theme of abundance, Green points out, was also profoundly important and found expression in Henri Le Fauconnier's elaborate allegory of fruitfulness and regeneration, *L'Abondance,* and Léger's *Etude pour une abondance.* René Arcos's *Ce qui naît* is evidence of the poets' concern with this theme, as is the section *Parole devant la femme enceinte* from Alexandre Mercereau's *Parole devant la vie.* What is missing in Green's discussion of these themes is a consideration of their political implications. The proliferation of images of Madonna and Child after the war is dealt with as another image of abundance. The return to representation in painting, the revival of neoclassicism, the homage paid to Jean Auguste Ingres and the general *rappel à l'ordre* after the war is seen as a "progressive move backwards" or another example of artistic novelty that once again illustrates the protean genius of the artist. No mention is made of the reactionary climate that conditioned this return to the old verities.

As well as these books, there are a number of essays that are relevant to this study. *Literature and the Plastic Arts 1880–1930* is a collection of seven essays edited by Ian Higgins. The historical period was chosen specifically because it is Higgins's belief that "the relation between the linguistic and the plastic arts came to acquire particular importance for artists during the period."[11] Of the seven essays, the most pertinent to our investigation are George Noszlopy's discussion of Apollinaire's aesthetics, Ulrich Finke's examination of Kurt Schwitters's contribution to the development of concrete poetry, and Anne Hyde Greet's analysis of five of Paul Eluard's poems on painters. The discussion of Apollinaire, in some ways the most influential and avant-garde writer considered here, is oddly paradoxical in that Noszlopy places Apollinaire's poems with cubist paintings in terms of allegorical themes and imagery. In the discussion of Paul Eluard's poems on painters, Greet mentions Eluard's interest in the techniques used by the painters (irrational juxtapositions, automatism, dream images, collage, and *frottage*) that in some cases correspond to the techniques of literary surrealism, but she does not develop these comparisons. Instead, the primary focus of this essay is on similarities of theme and subject matter. In his essay on Schwitters's poetry and his "*Merz*-pictures," Finke delineates the way in which language in Schwitters's work developed its own concreteness or plasticity and became indistinguishable from any other object on the canvas:

> In his pictures of 1919–21 Schwitters deals mainly with the superimposition of the functional and formal structure of the writing; later he reduced its functional structure in favour of its formal structure. "Sense-less" word fragments, meant to be typographic signs, are perceived entirely by conceptual, rather than the merely visual intellectuality of the eye. A similar tendency can be seen in his writing, where he dissolves the descriptive and representative function of the word, which enables him to arrive at picture-poems, or pure number or letter poems....[12]

Encounters, edited by John Dixon Hunt, is another collection of essays on literature and the visual arts. Unlike Higgins's collection, which focuses on the modern period, the essays in *Encounters* span a period of literary history extending from Piers Plowman to Wallace Stevens. There is no intended homogeneous critical method or comparativist criteria informing these essays except the most rudimentary principle—the idea of the *Zeitgeist*. The essay dealing with the modern period is Bram Dijkstra's "Wallace Stevens and William Carlos Williams: Poetry, Painting and the Function of Reality." Dijkstra's argument is that Stevens's involvement with the visual arts was ultimately destructive because Stevens used paintings as a substitute for reality, whereas Williams's involvement with the visual arts led him to a keener appreciation of reality.

One of the most interesting comparative essays is Rainer Crone's "Malevich and Khlebnikov: Suprematism Reinterpreted," which appeared in *Artforum* in 1978. Crone counters the standard interpretations of Malevich's painting and Khlebnikov's poetry by illustrating the influence they had on each other and their mutual interest in new scientific developments, particularly non-Euclidean geometry and the theories of the fourth dimension. Usually, the artistic development of Malevich is explained by way of formal steps, from Italian futurism to French cubism to his break with the mimesis of occidental art in *Black Square*. However, Crone argues that the origins of Malevich's abstractionism should not be sought in an internal consistency of a formal genesis (as with Piet Mondrian for example) but in extrapictorial stimulations, in the context of his fellow poets and their poetic theories. According to Crone, Malevich's sudden step into the nonobjective world, into pure geometrical forms, developed out of the impetus of Malevich's immediate cultural environment, "in the widely respected personality of Khlebnikov, a dominating figure of these years, and in the relationship between art and science as manifest specifically in the relation of Khlebnikov's poetry to mathematics."[13] Khlebnikov was originally a mathematician and as Crone points out:

> Just as mathematicians like Poincaré, Jouffret and others—besides such well-known authors as Apollinaire, Bergson, Mallarmé and Denis—had a significant influence on the development of French Cubists, so Khlebnikov played an analogous role for the Russian avant-garde. His poetic preoccupation with the "autonomous value" of the word as such— the "autotelic word," as he himself termed it, the "zaum-language" or "transrational language" could be explained, as it often is, from the tradition of Rimbaud, Mallarmé, French and Russian symbolism, or of Potebyna, the famous Russian linguist. But we must also take into account analogous developments in mathematics, geometry and arithmetic— an area to which Khlebnikov devoted particular attention in his utilization of numbers as semantic unities and, thus, as a means for poetic language. (41)

Crone's study is particularly helpful because of its broader, more inclusive investigation of the artistic and intellectual influences producing radical changes in literary form.

Marianne Martin's "Futurism, Unanimism, and Apollinaire" is important not only for its illustration of the links between the Abbaye de Creteil poets, the futurist poets, and the cubist poets, but for its analysis of some of the basic formative notions underlying the arts in general. She discusses the new theories in philosophy (Henri Bergson particularly), the current studies in visual perception, and the evolution of a new attitude to the machine age; and she relates these to the growing urge on the part of poets and painters to celebrate *l'esprit nouveau* of the modern era. Some of the analogies Martin makes are extremely provocative. For example, she parallels the painter's proposal to place the artist—and by extension the spectator—in the center of the canvas to Jules Romains's reputed artistic point of departure, what she describes as "his epochal experience on the crowded rue d'Amsterdam when he suddenly became aware of a vast and elemental being, of which the streets, the carriages and pedestrians formed the body, and of which he was the consciousness."[14] She points out that Boccioni and Carlo Carrà mention similar visual, almost visionary, experiences as the basis for their radical shift in location of the artist's perspective. She also suggests that Marinetti's *Technical Manifesto of Literature*—with its theory of analogies that replaced conventional syntax, punctuation, and the classical unities of location and time—reflects, in many respects, the painter's concept of "painting states of mind."

A 1986 anthology edited by Monique Chefdor, Ricardo Quinones, and Albert Wachtel entitled *Modernism: Challenges and Perspectives* is indicative of the kinds of criticism currently being undertaken on modernism and postmodernism. The collection brings together five disciplines (language, history of art, music, drama, and history), and almost all the essays are interdisciplinary in nature. What this anthology and the preceding brief survey I have provided reveal is that a revolution in critical thinking has taken place within this century. The century opened with wide acclaim for Irving Babbitt's *The New Laokoön* of 1910, which denied the possibility of interartistic similarity, yet it is coming to a close with the understanding that the only way to take the measure of the modernist achievement is by bringing together a variety of viewpoints from international and interdisciplinary perspectives.

Notes

Chapter 1

1. This error is noted by Bram Dijkstra, *The Hieroglyphics of a New Speech: Cubism, Stieglitz and the Early Poetry of William Carlos Williams* (Princeton: Princeton Univ. Press, 1969), ix.

2. J. Mitchell Morse, "Karl Gutzkow and the Novel of Simultaneity," *James Joyce Quarterly* 2 (1964), 13.

3. Christopher Gray, *Cubist Aesthetic Theories* (Baltimore: Johns Hopkins Press, 1953), 3.

4. Clement Greenberg, *Art and Culture: Critical Essays* (Boston: Beacon Press, 1969), 6.

5. Roland Barthes, *Writing Degree Zero and Elements of Semiology*, trans. Annette Lavers and Colin Smith (Boston: Beacon Press, 1970), 68.

6. Fredric Jameson, *Fables of Aggression: Wyndham Lewis, The Modernist as Fascist* (Berkeley: Univ. of California Press, 1979), 75–76.

7. Jean-François Lyotard, *The Post-Modern Condition: A Report on Knowledge*, trans. Geoff Bennington and Brian Massumi (Minneapolis: Univ. of Minnesota Press, 1984).

8. See Roman Jakobson, *Questions de poétique* (Paris: Editions du Seuil, 1973), 28, for a discussion of Einstein's theories as they apply to contemporary painting.

9. Jameson, *Fables of Aggression*, 3.

10. Wyndham Lewis, *Blasting and Bombardiering* (London: Eyre and Spottiswoode, 1937), 3.

11. Wyndham Lewis, *The Tyro, A Review of Art and Literature* 1–2 (London: Egoist Press, 1921–22).

12. Ford Madox Ford, *Thus to Revisit: Some Reminiscences of Ford Madox Hueffer* (London: Chapman and Hall, 1921), 174.

13. Arnold Bennett, "Neo-Impressionism in Literature," *The New Age* (December 8, 1910), reprinted in *Books and Persons* (London: Chatto and Windus, 1912).

14. Wyndham Lewis, *Rude Assignment, A Narrative of My Career Up-to-Date* (London: Hutchinson, 1950), 128–29.

15. Ezra Pound, *Gaudier-Brzeska: A Memoir* (New York: New Directions, 1960), 81.

16. Ezra Pound, "Vorticism" (1), *Fortnightly Review* 573 (September 1, 1914), 466.

17. Wyndham Lewis, "The Vorticists," *Vogue* (September 1956), 216.

18. Wilhelm Worringer, *Abstraction and Empathy: A Contribution to the Psychology of Style* (1908), trans. Michael Bullock (New York: International Universities Press, [1967]), 16–17.

19. This lecture was published in T.E. Hulme, *Speculations: Essays on Humanism and the Philosophy of Art,* ed. Herbert Read (London: K. Paul, Trench, Trubner, 1924), 82. For an account of the connections between Kandinsky and Worringer, see Will Grohmann, *Wassily Kandinsky* (Cologne: Du Mont Schauberg, 1961), and Peg Weiss, *Kandinsky in Munich* (New Jersey, 1979).

20. Lewis, *Blast* (1914), 48.

21. Gaudier-Brzeska, *Blast* (1914), 34.

22. Lewis, *Blasting and Bombardiering,* 106.

23. Lewis, *Blast,* 30 and 39.

24. Ezra Pound, "Prolegomena," *Poetry Review* 1 (February 1912).

25. Pound, "Vorticism."

26. Ezra Pound to the editor of *Poetry* (March 30, 1913). *The Letters of Ezra Pound,* ed. D.D. Paige (London: Faber and Faber, 1951), 53.

27. Wyndham Lewis, "A Review of Contemporary Art," *Blast* 2 (July 1915), 47.

28. Michel Foucault, "What Is an Author?" in *Textual Strategies: Perspectives in Post-Structuralist Criticism,* ed. Josué V. Harari (Ithaca: Cornell Univ. Press, 1979), 141.

29. James Joyce, *Ulysses* (New York: Modern Library, 1946), 205.

30. Edward Sapir, *Selected Writings in Language, Culture and Personality,* ed. David G. Mandelbaum (Berkeley: Univ. of California Press, 1949), 162.

31. Umberto Eco, *La struttura assente: Introduzione alla ricerca semiologica* (Milan: Bompiani, 1968), 113ff.

32. Peter Brooks, "Freud's Masterplot," *Yale French Studies,* 55 (1977), 299.

33. Jacques Lacan, *The Language of the Self: The Function of Language in Psychoanalysis,* trans. Anthony Wilden (Baltimore: Johns Hopkins Press, 1968), 183–84.

34. Fredric Jameson, *The Prison House of Language: A Critical Account of Structuralism and Russian Formalism* (Princeton: Princeton Univ. Press, 1972), 138.

35. Julia Kristeva, *Revolution in Poetic Language,* trans. Margaret Waller (New York: Columbia Univ. Press, 1984), 29.

36. Julia Kristeva, *Recherches pour une sémanalyse* (Paris: Editions du Seuil, 1969), 178–79.

37. Jameson, *Prison House of Language,* 140.

38. Barthes, *Writing Degree Zero,* 49.

39. Roland Barthes, *Critique et vérité* (Paris: Editions du Seuil, 1966), 46.

40. Roland Barthes, "To Write: An Intransitive Verb?" in *The Structuralist Controversy: The Languages of Criticism and the Sciences of Man,* ed. Richard Macksey and Eugenio Donato (Baltimore: Johns Hopkins Press, 1972), 144.

41. Julia Kristeva, *Desire in Language: A Semiotic Approach to Literature and Art*, ed. Leon S. Roudiez, trans. Thomas Gora, Alice Jardine and Leon S. Roudiez (New York: Columbia Univ. Press, 1980), 128.

42. Roland Barthes, *S/Z* (1970), trans. Richard Miller (New York: Hill and Wang, 1974), 4.

43. Besides its sexual implications, *jouissance* in this context can be described as joyous epistemological investigation. Barthes clarifies the ideological implications of *jouissance*:

   > An entire minor mythology would have us believe that pleasure (and singularly the pleasure of the text) is a rightist notion. On the right, with the same movement, everything abstract, boring, political, is shoved over to the left and pleasure is kept for oneself: welcome to our side, you who are finally coming to the pleasure of literature! And on the left, because of morality (forgetting Marx's and Brecht's cigars), one suspects and disdains any "residue of hedonism." On the right, pleasure is championed *against* intellectuality, the clerisy: the old reactionary myth of heart against head, sensation against reasoning, (warm) "life" against (cold) "abstraction": must not the artist, according to Debussy's sinister precept, *"humbly seek to give pleasure"?* On the left, knowledge, method, commitment, combat, are drawn up against "mere delectation" (and yet: what if knowledge itself were *delicious?*). On both sides, this peculiar idea that pleasure is *simple*, which is why it is championed or disdained. Pleasure, however, is not an element of the text, it is not a naive residue; it does not depend on a logic of understanding and on sensation; it is a drift, something both revolutionary and asocial, and it cannot be taken over by any collectivity, any mentality, any ideolect. Something *neuter?* It is obvious that the pleasure of the text is scandalous: not because it is immoral but because it is *atopic.* (Roland Barthes, *The Pleasure of the Text,* trans. Richard Miller [New York: Hill and Wang, 1975], 27.)

44. Roland Barthes, *Critical Essays,* trans. Richard Howard (Evanston: Northwestern Univ. Press, 1972), xvi.

45. Barthes, *The Pleasure of the Text,* 14.

46. Kristeva, *Desire in Language,* 139.

47. Barthes adopts what he calls "this admirable expression" from Arab scholars who, when speaking of the text, speak of "the certain body." Barthes asks and answers the question "Does the text have human form, is it a figure, an anagram of the body? Yes, but of our erotic body. . . . The pleasure of the text is that moment when my body pursues its own ideas—for my body does not have the same ideas I do." *The Pleasure of the Text,* 17.

48. Julia Kristeva, *About Chinese Women,* trans. Anita Barrows (London: Marion Boyars, 1977), 29.

49. Kristeva, *Desire in Language,* 146.

50. Ibid. and x.

Chapter 2

1. Richard Ellmann, *James Joyce* (New York: Oxford Univ. Press, 1959), 505.

2. See Betty M. Foley, "The Ubicubist Joyce," *Ball State University Forum,* 17 (Autumn 1976), 41–45; and Archie K. Loss, "Interior and Exterior Imagery in the Earlier Works of Joyce and Symbolist Art," *Journal of Modern Literature* 8, 1 (1950), 99–117.

3. Frank Budgen, *Myselves When Young* (London: Oxford Univ. Press, 1970), 187.

4. Ellmann, *James Joyce,* 754, 443.

5. Gertrude Stein, *The Autobiography of Alice B. Toklas* (New York: Harcourt, Brace, [1933]), 143.

6. James Joyce, *Stephen Hero, A Part of the First Draft of "A Portrait of the Artist as a Young Man,"* ed. Theodore Spencer (New York: New Directions, 1944), 33.

7. Gotthold Ephraim Lessing, *Laocoön: An Essay on the Limits of Painting and Poetry,* trans. Edward Allen McCormick (Indianapolis: Bobbs-Merrill, 1962). Lessing's theories, as a number of critics have pointed out, are not original, but his was the first attempt to use them systematically as an instrument of critical analysis. See Irving Babbitt, *The New Laokoon: An Essay on the Confusion of the Arts* (New York: Houghton, Mifflin, 1910), ch. 3.

8. Wassily Kandinsky, *The Spiritual in Art, and Painting in Particular,* trans. M.T.H. Sadleir, (1912), reprinted in *The Documents of Modern Art* (New York: Wittenborn, Schultz, 1947), 60.

9. Joseph Frank, "Spatial Form in Modern Literature," *Sewanee Review* 53 (1945), 226.

10. Ibid.

11. Cited in Herschel B. Chipp, comp., *Theories of Modern Art: A Source Book by Artists and Critics* (Berkeley: Univ. of California Press, 1968), 329.

12. Guillaume Apollinaire, *The Cubist Painters: Aesthetic Meditations,* trans. Lionel Abel (New York: Wittenborn, Schultz, 1944), 25.

13. For this reference I am indebted to Stewart Buettner, "An American Artist Elucidated Cubist Space: Max Weber on the Fourth Dimension," unpublished paper presented to the College Art Association of America, New York, 1978.

14. Cited in Robert L. Herbert, ed. *Modern Artists on Art* (Englewood Cliffs, New Jersey: Prentice-Hall, 1964).

15. Albert Einstein, *The Meaning of Relativity: Four Lectures Delivered at Princeton, 1921,* trans. Edward Plimpton Adams (Princeton: Princeton Univ. Press, 1923), 33.

16. For the argument against relativity's playing a significant role in the development of cubism see Linda Henderson, "New Facets of Cubism: The Fourth Dimension and Non-Euclidean Geometry," *Art Quarterly* 34, 4 (1971), 410–33.

17. Leo Stein, *Journey into the Self: Being the Letters, Papers and Journals of Leo Stein,* ed. Edmund Fuller (New York: Crown, 1950), 123.

18. Roger Shattuck, *The Banquet Years: The Arts in France 1895–1918* (London: Faber and Faber, 1959), 170.

19. Alfred Jarry, *Selected Works,* ed. Roger Shattuck and Simon Watson Taylor (London: Cape, 1965), 143.

20. Maurice Merleau-Ponty, "Cezanne's Doubt," in *Sense and Non-Sense,* trans. Hubert L. Dreyfus and Patricia Allen Dreyfus (Evanston: Northwestern Univ. Press, 1964), 14.

21. Georges Braque, "La Peinture et nous," in John Goulding, *Cubism: A History and an Analysis 1907–1914* (London: Faber and Faber, 1959), 85.

22. Scholars do not agree that all cubists were attempting to incorporate the element of time into their canvases, nor that futurism elaborated on the time concept of cubism. Guy Habasque cautions that "we should not lend too much credence to the theory that Picasso and Braque were likewise trying to represent movement by a static displacement of lines or the juxtaposition of successive views of the same object." He does agree that Albert Gleizes and Jean Metzinger, at least, were trying to express movement by these means. Guy Habasque, *Cubism: Biographical and Critical Study,* trans. Stuart Gilbert (Geneva: Skira, 1959), 122.

23. Cited in Robert Goldwater and Marco Treves, eds., *Artists on Art, From the XIV to the XX Century* (New York: Pantheon Books, 1945), 435.

24. For an account of the extent to which James utilized the visual arts see Viola Hopkins, "Visual Art Devices and Parallels in the Fiction of Henry James," *PMLA* 76 (1961), 561–74; and Adeline R. Tintner, *The Museum World of Henry James* (Ann Arbor, Michigan: UMI Research Press, 1986).

25. Cited in Marianne Martin, *Futurist Art and Theory* (Oxford: Clarendon, 1968), 109.

26. Paul M. Laporte, "The Space-Time Concept in the Work of Picasso," *Magazine of Art* 40 (1947), 26.

27. Leo Steinberg, "The Philosophical Brothel," *Art News* 71 (1972), 21.

28. Cited in Goldwater and Treves, *Artists on Art,* 435.

29. Gertrude Stein, *Picasso* (London: Batsford, 1939), 12. (Original publication, 1912).

30. James Joyce, *A Portrait of the Artist as a Young Man* (New York: Viking, 1964), 214–15 (emphasis mine).

31. Julia Kristeva, "The Ruin of a Poetics," *20th Century Studies* (December 1972), 111.

32. Cited in Goldwater and Treves, *Artists on Art,* 419.

33. Cited in Frank Budgen, *James Joyce and the Making of "Ulysses"* (New York: Smith and Hass, 1934), 67.

34. Robert Rosenblum, *Cubism and Twentieth-Century Art* (New York: Abrams, 1966), 7.

35. Cited in Chipp, *Theories of Modern Art,* 231.

36. Cited in Chipp, *Theories of Modern Art,* 260 (emphasis mine).

37. James Joyce, *Ulysses* (New York: Random House, 1961), 697; hereafter cited as *U.*

38. Bram Dijkstra, *Hieroglyphics,* 75.

39. For a discussion of this aspect of cubism see Habasque, *Cubism,* 52. The futurists took over this technique and gave it a philosophical rationale. (See Chipp, *Theories of Modern Art,* 209).

40. Budgen, *James Joyce,* 42.

41. Armin Arnold, *James Joyce* (New York: Ungar, 1969), 42.

42. Budgen, *James Joyce,* 185.

43. Ibid., 156.

44. Cited in Goldwater and Treves, *Artists on Art,* 435.

45. Morse, "Karl Gutzkow," 13. Morse's claim that Joyce was familiar with the work is based on the appearance of the terms *Nacheinander* and *Nebeneinander* in the Proteus episode. These terms, Morse says, were first applied to the special problems of novel writing by Gutzkow. Joyce does not use the terms in this context, however, and the terms themselves Joyce would have encountered in Lessing's *Laocoön,* a work he knew well.

46. Guillaume Apollinaire, "Simultanisme-Librettisme," *Les Soirées de Paris* (June 15, 1914), 324–25.

47. *291* 1–12 (1915–16) (New York: Arno Press, 1972).

48. Cited in Chipp, *Theories of Modern Art,* 303.

49. For these examples I am indebted to Martin, *Futurist Art and Theory,* 162–63.

50. Stéphane Mallarmé, preface, *Un Coup de dés jamais n'abolira le hasard* (1897), trans. Daisy Ablan, *Folder* 4 (1956), Tiber Press.

51. Gerald Brun, "Mallarmé: The Transcendence of Language and the Aesthetics of the Book," *The Journal of Typographic Research* 3 (July 1969), 230.

52. Robert Rosenblum, "Picasso and the Typography of Cubism," in *Picasso in Retrospect,* ed. Roland Penrose and John Golding (New York: Praeger, 1973), 50.

53. Herbert Gorman, *James Joyce* (New York: Farrar & Rinehart, 1939), 185.

54. Rosenblum, "Picasso," 75.

55. Cited in Chipp, *Theories of Modern Art,* 262.

56. Cited in Habasque, *Cubism,* 142.

57. Rosenblum, *Cubism,* 66.

58. See Budgen, *James Joyce,* 22, and Joyce, *Portrait,* 166, for references to Joyce's interest in the materiality of language.

59. William Carlos Williams, *Autobiography* (New York: New Directions, 1951), 380.

60. William Barrett, *Irrational Man: A Study on Existential Philosophy* (Garden City, New York: Doubleday, 1962).

61. See Gray, *Cubist Aesthetic Theories,* 19.

62. Alain Robbe-Grillet, *Snapshots, and, Towards a New Novel,* trans. Barbara Wright (London: Calder & Boyars, 1965), 151.

63. Cited in Chipp, 277.

64. Arnold Hauser, *The Social History of Art,* trans. Stanley Godman (New York: Vintage, 1958), 230.

65. Cited in Chipp.

Chapter 3

1. The manifesto was signed by R. Aldington, Arbuthnot, L. Atkinson, H. Gaudier-Brzeska, J. Dismorr, C. Hamilton, E. Pound, W. Roberts, H. Sanders, E. Wadsworth and Wyndham Lewis.

2. The manifesto was signed by David Burliuk, Aleksei Kruchenykh, Vladimir Mayakovsky and Victor Khlebnikov. English translation Vladimir Markov, *Russian Futurism—A History* (London: MacGibbon & Kee, 1969), 45–46. The term futurist causes some

confusion in the context of the Russian avant-garde. It is not synonymous with Italian futurism from which the Russians dissociated themselves, nor was the term borrowed from the Italians. It is an abbreviation of "Men of the Future," which the group of Russians had called themselves prior to the inception of Italian futurism.

3. Walter Pater, "The School of Giorgione," in *The Renaissance* (1873) (New York: Modern Library, 1961), 129, 128 and 132. Actually, Pound misquotes Pater. The sentence should read "All art constantly aspires towards the condition of music."

4. Kazimir Malevich, "On New Systems in Art," in *Essays on Art 1915–1935*, ed. Troels Andersen, trans. Xenia Glowacki-Prus and Arnold McMillen (London: Rapp & Whiting, 1969), 1:92.

5. This phrase became the title of their 1913 manifesto.

6. Aleksei Kruchenykh in *Troe [The Three]* (Moscow: Zhuravl, 1913), trans. Susan P. Compton, *The World Backwards: Russian Futurist Books 1912–1916* (London: British Library, 1978), 56 (my italics).

7. Benedikt Livshits, "Liberation of the Word," in *The Crooked Moon* (Moscow: Osyen, 1914). Quoted in Susan P. Compton, "Malevich's Suprematism—the Higher Intuition," *Burlington Magazine* 118 (August 1976): 577–85.

8. Ezra Pound, *Literary Essays of Ezra Pound*, ed. T.S. Eliot (London: Faber and Faber, 1954), 11.

9. Roman Jakobson, "What Is Poetry?" in *Questions de poétique* (Paris: Editions du Seuil, 1973), 122.

10. T.S. Eliot, *"Ulysses,* Order, and Myth," *The Dial* 75 (1923): 480–83.

11. Ezra Pound, *Hugh Selwyn Mauberley* (London: Ovid Press, 1920).

12. For a detailed analysis of the connections between "mass" and "high" culture see Renato Poggioli, *The Spirit of the Letter: Essays in European Literature* (Cambridge: Harvard Univ. Press, 1965).

13. Ezra Pound, *Make It New: Essays* (London: Faber and Faber, 1934); but the essay as a whole must be dated 1910–31.

14. Ezra Pound, "Vortex," *Blast* 1 (1914): 154.

15. Roman Jakobson, "Modern Russian Poetry: Velimir Khlebnikov," trans. Edward J. Brown, in *Major Soviet Writers: Essays in Criticism,* ed. Edward J. Brown (London: Oxford Univ. Press, 1973), 58–82.

16. Ezra Pound, "Brancusi" (1921), in *Literary Essays of Ezra Pound,* 441. Pound is quoting T.J. Everest and claims that this statement is "the best summary of our contemporary aesthetics."

17. Quoted in Jakobson, "Modern Russian Poetry," 61.

18. Ezra Pound, interview with Zinaida Vengerova, "Angliiskie futuristy," *Strelets* 1 (1915): 93–94. Unpublished translation by John Barnstead.

19. Friedrich Nietzsche, *Der Wille zur Macht: Versuch einer Umwerthung aller Werthe* (Leipzig: Naumann, 1901). Cited in Christopher Middleton, *Bolshevism in Art and Other Expository Writings* (Manchester: Carcanet New Press, 1978), 285.

20. *Blast* 1 (1914): 119–25, trans. Edward Wadsworth.

21. Pound, "The New Sculpture," *The Egoist* 1 (February 16, 1914).

22. This connection is pointed out by Richard Cork, *Vorticism and Abstract Art in the First Machine Age* (Berkeley: Univ. of California Press, 1976). I am also indebted to Cork for pointing out the connections between Rodchenko and Bomberg's compass drawings (see figures 16 and 17).

23. Markov, *Russian Futurism,* 34.

24. This was one of the tenets of the Knave of Diamonds, an exhibition society established by Mikhail Larionov and Natalya Goncharova. For an exploration of Russian primitivism see John E. Bowlt, "Neo-primitivism and Russian Painting," *Burlington Magazine* 116 (March 1974), 113–39. I am indebted to Professor Bowlt for the preceding information.

25. Cited in Bowlt, "Neo-Primitivism," 134.

26. Peter Lieven, *The Birth of Ballets-Russes,* 1936, trans. L. Zarine (London: Allen & Unwin, 1956), 106.

27. Quoted in Lieven, *The Birth of Ballets-Russes,* 159. Wyndham Lewis was provoked to write a critique of Diaghileff's ballets in which he criticizes Diaghileff for associating the "finest artist of his time" with the "art of this High Bohemia of the revolutionary rich." He reserves his praise for Diaghileff's early "primitive" ballets. "The Russian Ballet, the Most Perfect Expression of the High Bohemia," in *The Enemy: A Review of Art and Literature,* 1927–29); reprint (New York: Kraus Reprint, 1967), 54–57.

28. Mikhail Larionov, "Rayonist Manifesto" (Moscow, 1913), quoted in Camilla Gray, *The Russian Experiment in Art, 1863–1922* (London: Thames and Hudson, 1962), 138.

29. Quoted in "A Neglected Phase of British Art," editorial, *Apollo* (March 1917), 182.

30. Roger Fry, "M. Larionov and the Russian Ballet," *Burlington Magazine* 34 (1919), 112–18.

31. "The Omega Workshops Ltd.," in *Catalogue of the Ideal Home Exhibition* (London: *Daily Mail,* 1913), 195.

32. Boris Arvatov, *Iskusstvo i proizvodstvo* (Moscow: Proletcult, 1926), 95. Unpublished translation by Nathan Smith.

33. Kazimir Malevich to Alexander Benois, May 1916, in *Essays on Art,* 1:45.

34. Kazimir Malevich, *The Non-Objective World* (1926), trans. Howard Dearstyne (Chicago: P. Theobald, 1959), 74.

35. See Linda Henderson, "The Merging of Time and Space: 'The Fourth Dimension' in Russia from Ouspensky to Malevich," *The Structurist* 15/16 (1975/76), 87–108; Compton, "Malevich's Suprematism," 577–85; and Rainer Crone, "Malevich and Khlebnikov: Suprematism Reinterpreted," *Artforum* (December 1978), note 6.

36. See Boris Uspensky, *The Semiotics of the Russian Icon,* ed. Stephen Rudy, trans. P.A. Reed, 1922, reprint (Lisse: P. de Ridder Press, 1976).

37. Jacques Derrida, *Positions: Entretiens avec Henri Ronse, Julia Kristeva, Jean-Louis Houdebine, Guy Scarpetta* (Paris: Editions de Minuit, 1972), 23–25.

38. Cited in Crone, "Malevich and Khlebnikov," 43.

39. Malevich, *Essays on Art,* 1:90.

40. Malevich, cited in Crone, "Malevich and Khlebnikov," 40.

41. See Crone, "Malevich and Khlebnikov" and Charlotte Douglas, "Birth of a 'Royal Infant': Malevich and Victory over the Sun," *Art in America* 62 (March/April 1974), 45–63.

42. Kolia Tomaskevsky, "Vladimir Mayakovsky," *Teatr* 4 (1938), trans. Ewa Bartos and Victoria Nes Kirby in *TDR/The Drama Review* 15 (Fall 1971): 99–101. The image of Heliomachia is also found in other early poems by Mayakovsky and in Khlebnikov's writings. See Markov, *Russian Futurism,* 399.

43. Markov, *Russian Futurism,* 154.

44. Wyndham Lewis, *Rude Assignment,* 129.

45. Markov, *Russian Futurism,* 146.

46. Wyndham Lewis, "Enemy of the Stars," *Blast* 1 (1914): 60; hereafter cited as *E.*

47. *Victory over the Sun,* trans. by Ewa Bartos and Victoria Nes Kirby, *TDR/The Drama Review* 15, (Fall 1971), 121; hereafter cited as *V.*

48. Benedikt Livshits, *Polutoraglazyi Strelets* (Leningrad, 1933), 187–88; cited in Compton, *The World Backwards.*

49. This is Fredric Jameson's description of Lewis's characters, *Fables of Aggression,* 44.

50. This is from the 1932 version of the play (London: Harmsworth, 1932), 40.

51. *Victory over the Sun.* Cited in Camilla Gray, *The Russian Experiment,* 186.

52. M. Matyushin, "Futurizm v peterburge," *Futuristy: Pervyi jhurnal russkikh futuristov* 1–2 (1914), 156; cited in Douglas, "Birth of a 'Royal Infant,'" 48.

53. Ibid., 47.

54. Julia Kristeva, *Desire in Language,* 78–79 (emphasis mine).

55. Jakobson, "Modern Russian Poetry," 75.

56. This phrase, made popular by Ortega y Gasset, was first used by Wyndham Lewis in *Blast* 1:141 to describe his aesthetic intent.

57. Joseph Riddell, "Decentering the Image: The Project of 'American' Poetics?" in *Textual Strategies: Perspectives in Post-Structuralist Criticism,* ed. Josué V. Harari (Ithaca: Cornell Univ. Press, 1979), 325–45.

58. Kristeva, *Desire in Language,* 79.

59. Wyndham Lewis, *The Letters of Wyndham Lewis,* ed. W.K. Rose (London: Methuen, 1963), 552. This is what Lewis had hoped *Tarr* (written in the same year as *Enemy of the Stars*) would be.

60. Hugh Kenner, *Wyndham Lewis: The Makers of Modern Literature* (London: Methuen, 1954), 16.

61. Lewis, *Rude Assignment,* 129.

62. Lewis, *Letters,* 69.

63. Lewis, *Rude Assignment,* 129.

64. Lewis, *Blasting and Bombardiering,* 35.

65. Lewis, *The Demon of Progress in the Arts* (London: Methuen, 1954), 3.

66. Christopher Nevinson, interview in *New York Times* (May 1919); interview in *The Studio* (December 1919). Both interviews cited in Richard Cork, *Vorticism and Abstract Art in the First Machine Age* (Berkeley: Univ. of California Press, 1976), 2: 512.

67. Ezra Pound to William Carlos Williams, September 11, 1920, *The Letters of Ezra Pound*, 223.

68. Wyndham Lewis, *The Caliph's Design: Architects! Where Is Your Vortex?* (London: Egoist, 1919), 29 and 7.

69. El Lissitzky, "The Book," in *El Lissitzky: Life, Letters, Texts*, ed. Sophie Lissitzky-Küppers (London, 1980), 362.

70. *Declaration* (1921). For a detailed account of Russian imaginism see Renato Poggioli, "Imaginism and Ego-Futurism," in *The Poets of Russia 1890–1930* (Cambridge: Harvard Univ. Press, 1960).

71. Both Tatlin's and Mayakovsky's statements are from "Meeting ob iskusstve" in *Iskusstvo Kommuni* 1, (December 7, 1918); cited in Camilla Gray, *The Russian Experiment*, 219.

72. Alexander Rodchenko cited in German Karginov, *Rodchenko* (London: Thames and Hudson, 1979), 90.

73. Victor Khlebnikov, *A Teacher and Pupil*, 1912; cited in Markov, *Russian Futurism*, 40.

74. Malevich, "On New Systems in Art," in *Essays on Art*, 94.

75. Malevich, "The Problems of Art and the Role of Its Suppressors," *Essays on Art*, 49.

76. V.E. Tatlin, *Ezhednevnii Bulletin S'ezda*, 13 (1921): 11; cited in Camilla Gray, *The Russian Experiment*, 219.

Chapter 4

1. John Cage, *Silence: Lectures and Writings* (Cambridge: M.I.T. Press, 1961), 93.

2. Kenneth Rexroth, *Birds in the Bush: Obvious Essays* (New York: New Directions, 1959), 10.

3. Jan Mukařovský, "Standard Language and Poetic Language," in *A Prague School Reader on Esthetics, Literary Structure and Style*, ed. Paul L. Garvin (Washington: Georgetown Univ. Press, 1964), 23.

4. José Ortega y Gasset, *The Dehumanization of Art and Other Writings on Art and Culture*, trans. Willard A. Trask (Garden City, New York: Doubleday, 1956), 10.

5. Roland Barthes, "The Last Word on Robbe-Grillet?," in *Critical Essays*, 199.

6. Gertrude Stein, "Composition as Explanation," in *Selected Writings of Gertrude Stein*, ed. Carl Van Vechten (New York: Random House, [1946]), 453.

7. This phrase is from David Michael Levin, "The Novelhood of the Novel: The Limits of Representation and the Modernist Discovery of Presence," *Chicago Review* 28 (Spring 1977), 88. Levin's essay is a central document in this context.

8. Kristeva includes a cryptic, but provocative footnote on this subject: "It seems that what is persistently being called 'interior monologue' is the most indomitable way in which an entire civilization conceives itself as identity, as organized chaos, and finally, as transcendence. Yet, this 'monologue' probably exists only in texts that pretend to reconstitute the so-called physical reality of 'verbal flux.' Western man's state of 'interiority' is thus a limited literary effect (confessional form, continuous psychological speech, automatic writing). In a way, then, Freud's 'Copernican' revolution (the discovery of the split within the subject) put an end to the fiction of an internal voice by positing the fundamental principles governing the subject's radical exteriority in relation to, and within, language." *Desire in Language*, 80.

9. Walter Benjamin, "The Author as Producer," in *Reflections: Essays, Aphorisms, Autobiographical Writings,* ed. Peter Demetz (New York: Harcourt Brace Jovanovich, 1978), 235.

10. Walter Benjamin, *Illuminations,* ed. Hannah Arendt, trans. Harry Zohn (New York: Schocken Books, 1969), 254–55.

11. Gertrude Stein, *Autobiography,* 119.

12. Gertrude Stein, "Poetry and Grammar," in *Lectures in America* (New York: Random House, 1935), 237–38.

13. This was decoded by the editors of *transition* 3 (June 1927), 174.

14. Gertrude Stein, *Autobiography,* 212.

15. "K.O.R.A.A.," *transition* 3 (June 1927), 176.

16. Gertrude Stein, "A Transatlantic Interview 1946," in *A Primer for the Gradual Understanding of Gertrude Stein,* ed. Robert Bartlett Haas (Los Angeles: Black Sparrow Press, 1971), 18.

17. Tristan Tzara, *Seven Dada Manifestos and Lampisteries,* trans. Barbara Wright (London: Calder, 1977), 59.

18. Jacques Lacan, *Ecrits,* trans. Alan Sheridan (New York: W.W. Norton, 1977), 43.

19. Gertrude Stein, *The Geographical History of America or The Relation of Human Nature to the Human Mind,* 1933; reprint (New York: Vintage Books, 1973), 198–99.

20. Cited in John Golding, *Cubism: A History and Analysis, 1907–1914,* 2nd ed. (New York: Harper & Row, 1968), 93.

21. Gertrude Stein, *Autobiography,* 92.

22. Pierre Guiraud, *Semiology* (London and Boston: Routledge and Kegan Paul, 1975), 40.

23. Gertrude Stein, *Gertrude Stein on Picasso,* ed. Edward Burns (New York: Liveright, 1970), 48–53.

24. Gertrude Stein, *Primer,* 34.

25. Stein, "Poetry and Grammar," 215.

26. Gertrude Stein, "Portraits and Repetition," in *Lectures in America,* 196–97.

27. Marjorie Perloff, "Poetry as Word-System: The Art of Gertrude Stein," *The American Poetry Review* 8 (September/October 1979), 34. The scansion of the poem follows Perloff.

28. Virgil Thompson, *Virgil Thompson* (New York: Knopf, 1966), 90.

29. Gertrude Stein, "Poetry and Grammar," 231.

30. Carl Andre and Hollis Frampton, *12 Dialogues: 1962–1963* (Halifax: Press of the Nova Scotia College of Art and Design, 1980), 38.

31. Gertrude Stein, *Writings and Lectures 1911–45,* ed. Patricia Meyerowitz (London: Owen, 1967), 7.

32. Barthes, *Writing Degree Zero,* 84.

33. Kandinsky, *Concerning the Spiritual in Art,* 34.

34. Lacan, *Ecrits,* 54.

35. Gertrude Stein, "The Gradual Making of *The Making of Americans,*" in *Lectures in America,* 38.

36. Gertrude Stein, *Three Lives: Stories of the Good Anna, Melanctha, and the Gentle Lena* (New York: Random House, 1909), 226.

37. Roman Jakobson, "Two Aspects of Language and Two Types of Linguistic Disturbances," in Roman Jakobson and Morris Halle, *Fundamentals of Language* (The Hague: Mouton, 1956), 90. For a book-length discussion of Jakobson's theories as they apply to Stein's writing see Randa Kay Dubnick, *The Structure of Obscurity: Gertrude Stein, Language, and Cubism* (Urbana and Chicago: Univ. of Illinois Press, 1984).

38. Gertrude Stein, "Picasso," in *Selected Writings,* 293.

39. Gertrude Stein, "Poetry and Grammar," 209–10.

40. Guillaume Apollinaire, *The Cubist Painters: Aesthetic Meditations 1913,* trans. Lionel Abel (New York: Wittenborn, Schultz, Inc., 1949), 13.

41. Gertrude Stein, "A Transatlantic Interview," 15.

42. Gertrude Stein, "Picasso," 119.

43. Gertrude Stein, "Lecture 2," in *Narration: Four Lectures* (Chicago: Univ. of Chicago Press), 20.

44. Both Wendy Steiner and John Malcolm Brinnin discuss the parallels between analytic and synthetic cubism and Stein's stylistic changes. Wendy Steiner, *Exact Resemblance to Exact Resemblance: The Literary Portraiture of Gertrude Stein* (New Haven: Yale Univ. Press, 1978). John Malcom Brinnin, *The Third Rose: Gertrude Stein and Her World* (Boston: Little Brown, 1959).

45. Gertrude Stein, *Gertrude Stein on Picasso,* 43.

46. Gertrude Stein, "Poetry and Grammar," 134. To name something is to cause it to enter the realm of signification. Stein devised various modes of "refusal" to undermine those activities that "give meaning." In *A Novel of Thank You* she makes naming a totally arbitrary activity in which "Everybody is named Etienne. Everybody is named Charles. Everybody is named Alice" (New Haven: Yale Univ. Press, 1958), 43.

47. Gertrude Stein, "Poetry and Grammar," 235.

48. Gertrude Stein, "Tender Buttons," in *Writing and Lectures,* 181.

49. Gertrude Stein, "Portraits and Repetition," 191–92.

50. Gertrude Stein, "Pictures," in *Lectures in America,* 61.

51. Juan Gris, cited in Chipp, *Theories of Modern Art,* 274.

52. Edward F. Fry, ed., *Cubism* (London: Thames & Hudson, 1966), 39.

53. Octavio Paz, *Marcel Duchamp: Appearance Stripped Bare,* trans. Rachel Phillips and Donald Gardner (New York: Viking, [1978]), 21–22.

54. Levin, "The Novelhood of the Novel," 99.

55. Kristeva, *Desire in Language*, 151.

56. Walter Benjamin, "The Storyteller: Reflections on the Work of Nikolai Leskov," in *Illuminations*, 100–101.

57. This is a comment made by Dale E. Peterson in his analysis of Nabokov's *Invitation: Literature as Execution*," *PMLA* 96 (October 1981), 831. Peterson also provides an analysis of Benjamin's essay.

58. Gertrude Stein, *The Geographical History of America*, 150.

59. Gertrude Stein, "Portraits and Repetition," 189.

60. Gertrude Stein, *The Making of Americans, Being a History of a Family's Progress* (Paris: Contact, 1925); condensed ed. (New York: Harcourt, Brace, 1934), 294.

61. Barthes, *S/Z*, 16.

62. Barthes, *Writing Degree Zero*, 86–87.

63. William Carlos Williams, "A 1 Pound Stein," in *Selected Essays of William Carlos Williams* (New York: New Directions, 1954), 163.

Appendix

1. Mario Praz, *Mnemosyne: The Parallel between Literature and the Visual Arts* (Princeton: Princeton Univ. Press, 1967), 25.

2. Dickran Tashjian, *Skyscraper Primitives: Dada and the American Avant-Garde. 1910–1925* (Middletown, Connecticut: Wesleyan Univ. Press, 1975), xi.

3. Hart Crane, "Modern Poetry," *Complete Poems*, ed. Brom Weber (New York: Liveright, 1966), 261–62.

4. E.E. Cummings, *The Enormous Room* (New York: The Modern Library, 1934), 114.

5. Quoted in Wylie Sypher, *Rococo to Cubism in Art and Literature* (New York: Random House, 1960), xix.

6. Georges Lemaître, *From Cubism to Surrealism in French Literature* (New York: Ungar, 1967), 109.

7. Marcel Raymond, *From Baudelaire to Surrealism* (London: Methuen, 1970), 253. First published as *De Baudelaire au surréalisme*, 1933.

8. Gerald Kamber, *Max Jacob and the Poetics of Cubism* (Baltimore: Johns Hopkins Press, 1971), 41.

9. See for example: Marianne Dekoven, "Gertrude Stein and Modern Painting: Beyond Literary Cubism," *Contemporary Literature* 22 (1978), 81–95; Mabel Dodge, "Speculation, or Post-Impressionism in Prose," *Arts and Decoration* 3 (1913), 172–74; Earl Fendelman, "Gertrude Stein among the Cubists," *Journal of Modern Literature* 2 (November 1972), 481–90; L.T. Fitz, "Gertrude Stein and Picasso: The Language of Surfaces," *American Literature* 45 (1973), 228–37; Samuel H. McMillan, "Gertrude Stein, the Cubists and the Futurists," dissertation, Univ. of Texas, 1964; James R. Mellow, "Gertrude Stein among the Dadaists," *Arts Magazine* (May 1977), 124–27; Marjorie Perloff, "Poetry as Word-System:

The Art of Gertrude Stein," *The American Poetry Review* 8 (September/October 1979), 33–44; Marilyn Gaddis Rose, "Gertrude Stein and the Cubist Narrative," *Modern Fiction Studies* 22 (1967/77), 543–55; Neil Schmitz, "Gertrude Stein as Post-Modernist: The Rhetoric of *Tender Buttons*," *Journal of Modern Literature* 3 (1974), 1203–19; William Wasserstrom, "The Sursymamericubealism of Gertrude Stein," *Twentieth Century Literature* 21 (1975), 90–106.

10. From Léger's May 1913 Académie Wassilief lecture. Cited in Christopher Green, *Léger and the Avant-Garde* (New Haven: Yale Univ. Press, 1976), 73.

11. Ian Higgins, ed., *Literature and the Plastic Arts 1880–1930: Seven Essays* (New York: Barnes & Noble, 1973), v.

12. Ulrich Finke, "Kurt Schwitters' Contribution to Concrete Art and Poetry," in *Literature and the Plastic Arts 1880–1930,* ed. Ian Higgins, 78.

13. Crone, "Malevich and Khlebnikov," 39.

14. Marianne Martin, "Futurism, Unanimism, and Apollinaire," *Art Journal* 28–29 (1969), 259.

Bibliography

Andre, Carl, and Frampton, Hollis. *12 Dialogues: 1962–1963*. Halifax: Press of the Nova Scotia College of Art and Design, 1980.

Apollinaire, Guillaume. *Apollinaire on Art: Essays and Reviews, 1902–1918*. Edited by Le Roy C. Breunig. Translated by Susan Suleiman. New York: Viking, 1972.

———. *Calligrammes, Poèmes de la paix et de la guerre (1913–1916)*. 3rd ed. Paris: Gallimard, 1925.

———. *The Cubist Painters: Aesthetic Meditations*. Translated by Lionel Abel. New York: Wittenborn, Schultz, 1944.

———. "Simultanisme-Librettisme." *Les Soirées de Paris* 25 (June 15, 1914): 324–25.

Apollonio, Umbro, ed. *Futurist Manifestos*. London: Thames & Hudson, 1973.

Arnold, Armin. *James Joyce*. New York: Ungar, 1969.

Arvatov, Boris. *Iskusstvo i proizvodstvo*. Unpublished translation by Nathan Smith. Moscow: Proletcult, 1926.

Babbitt, Irving. *The New Laokoon: An Essay on the Confusion of the Arts*. New York: Houghton, Mifflin, 1910.

Balakian, Anna. *Literary Origins of Surrealism: A New Mysticism in French Poetry*. New York: King's Crown Press, 1947.

Barr, Alfred H. *Picasso: Fifty Years of His Art*. Boston: New York Graphic Society, 1974.

Barrett, William. *Irrational Man: A Study on Existential Philosophy*. Garden City, New York: Doubleday, 1962.

Barthes, Roland. *Critical Essays*. Translated by Richard Howard. Evanston: Northwestern University Press, 1972.

———. *Critique et vérité*. Paris: Editions du Seuil, 1966.

———. "The Last Word on Robbe-Grillet?" In *Critical Essays*. Translated by Richard Howard, pp. 197–204. Evanston: Northwestern University Press, 1972.

———. *The Pleasure of the Text*. Translated by Richard Miller. New York: Hill and Wang, 1975.

———. *S/Z*. Translated by Richard Miller. New York: Hill and Wang, 1974.

———. "To Write: An Intransitive Verb?" In *The Structuralist Controversy: The Languages of Criticism and the Sciences of Man*. Edited by Richard Macksey and Eugenio Donato. Baltimore: Johns Hopkins Press, 1972.

———. *Writing Degree Zero and Elements of Semiology*. Translated by Annette Lavers and Colin Smith. Boston: Beacon Press, 1970.

Bates, Scott. *Guillaume Apollinaire*. New York: Twayne, 1967.

Benjamin, Walter. "The Author as Producer." In Peter Demetz, ed., *Reflections: Essays, Aphorisms, Autobiographical Writings*. New York: Harcourt Brace Jovanovich, 1978.

———. *Illuminations*. Edited by Hannah Arendt. Translated by Harry Zohn. New York: Schocken Books, 1969.

Bennett, Arnold. "Neo-Impressionism in Literature." *The New Age* (December 8, 1910). Reprinted in *Books and Persons,* pp. 280–85. London: Chatto and Windus, 1917.

Berger, John. *The Moment of Cubism and Other Essays.* New York: Pantheon, 1969.

Blast: Review of the Great English Vortex. Nos. 1–12. London: J. Lane, June 20, 1914–July 1915.

Bowlt, John E. "Neo-primitivism and Russian Painting." *Burlington Magazine* 116 (March 1974): 133–39.

Bradbury, Malcolm, and McFarlane, James. *Modernism.* New York: Penguin, 1976.

Braque, Georges. "La Peinture et nous." In John Golding, *Cubism: A History and an Analysis, 1907–1914.* London: Faber and Faber, 1959.

Breunig, LeRoy C. *Guillaume Apollinaire.* Columbia Essays on Modern Writers, 46. New York: Columbia University Press, 1969.

Brinnin, John Malcolm. *The Third Rose: Gertrude Stein and Her World.* Boston: Little Brown, 1959.

Brooks, Peter. "Freud's Masterplot." *Yale French Studies* 55 (1977): 280–300.

Brun, Gerald. "Mallarmé: The Transcendence of Language and the Aesthetics of the Book." *The Journal of Typographic Research* 3 (July 1969): 219–40.

Budgen, Frank. *James Joyce and the Making of "Ulysses."* New York: Smith and Hass, 1934.

———. *Myselves When Young.* London: Oxford University Press, 1970.

Buettner, Stewart. "An American Artist Elucidated Cubist Space: Max Weber on the Fourth Dimension." Paper presented at the College Art Association of America, New York, 1978.

Cage, John. *Silence: Lectures and Writings.* Cambridge, Mass.: M.I.T. Press, 1961.

Carmody, Francis. *Cubist Poetry: The School of Apollinaire.* Berkeley: University of California Press, 1954.

Chefdor, Monique, Quinones, Ricardo, and Wachtel, Albert, eds. *Modernism: Challenges and Perspectives.* Urbana and Chicago: University of Illinois Press, 1986.

Chipp, Herschel B., comp. *Theories of Modern Art: A Source Book by Artists and Critics.* Berkeley: University of California Press, 1968.

Chomsky, Noam. "Some Methodological Remarks on Generative Grammar." *Word* 17 (1961): 219–39.

Compton, Susan P. "Malevich's Suprematism—The Higher Intuition." *Burlington Magazine* 118 (August 1976): 577–85.

———. *The World Backwards: Russian Futurist Books 1912–1916.* London: British Library, 1978.

Cooper, Douglas. *The Cubist Epoch.* Los Angeles: Phaidon, 1971.

Cork, Richard. *Vorticism and Abstract Art in the First Machine Age.* Berkeley: University of California Press, 1976.

Coward, Rosalind, and Ellis, John. *Language and Materialism: Developments in Semiology and the Theory of the Subject.* London: Routledge, Kegan Paul, 1977.

Crane, Hart. "Modern Poetry." In Brom Weber, ed., *Complete Poems.* New York: Liveright, 1966.

Crone, Rainer. "Malevich and Khlebnikov: Suprematism Reinterpreted." *Artforum* (December 1978): 38–50.

Culler, Jonathan D. *Structuralist Poetics: Structuralism, Linguistics, and the Study of Literature.* Ithaca: Cornell University Press, 1975.

Cummings, E.E. *The Enormous Room.* New York: The Modern Library, 1934.

Dekoven, Marianne. "Gertrude Stein and Modern Painting: Beyond Literary Cubism." *Contemporary Literature* 22 (1978): 81–95.

Derrida, Jacques. *Dissémination.* Translated, with an introduction, by Barbara Johnson. Chicago: University of Chicago Press, 1981.

———. *Of Grammatology.* Translated by Gayatri Chakravorty Spivak. Baltimore: Johns Hopkins University Press, 1976.

———. *Positions: Entretiens avec Henri Ronse, Julia Kristeva, Jean-Louis Houdebine, Guy Scarpetta.* Paris: Editions de Minuit, 1972.

Dijkstra, Bram. *The Hieroglyphics of a New Speech: Cubism, Stieglitz and the Early Poetry of William Carlos Williams.* Princeton: Princeton University Press, 1969.

Dodge, Mabel. "Speculation, or Post-Impressionism in Prose." *Arts and Decoration* 3 (1913): 172–74.

Douglas, Charlotte. "Birth of a 'Royal Infant': Malevich and *Victory over the Sun.*" *Art in America* 62 (March/April 1974): 45–63.

Dubnick, Randa Kay. *The Structure of Obscurity: Gertrude Stein, Language, and Cubism.* Urbana and Chicago: University of Illinois Press, 1984.

Eco, Umberto. *La struttura assente: Introduzione alla ricerca semiologica.* Milan: Bompiani, 1968.

———. *A Theory of Semiotics.* Bloomington: Indiana University Press, 1976.

Eddy, Arthur Jerome. *Cubists and Post-Impressionism.* Chicago: A.C. McClurg, 1919.

Einstein, Albert. *The Meaning of Relativity: Four Lectures Delivered at Princeton, 1921.* Translated by Edward Plimpton Adams. Princeton: Princeton University Press, 1923.

Eliot, T.S. "*Ulysses*, Order, and Myth." *The Dial* 75 (1923): 480–83.

Ellmann, Richard. *James Joyce.* New York: Oxford University Press, 1959.

Ellmann, Richard, and Feidelson, Charles, eds. *The Modern Tradition: Backgrounds of Modern Literature.* Oxford: Oxford University Press, 1965.

Erlich, Victor. *Russian Formalism: History-Doctrine.* 2nd ed. The Hague: Mouton, 1965.

Fendelman, Earl. "Gertrude Stein among the Cubists." *Journal of Modern Literature* 2 (November 1972): 481–90.

Fitz, L.T. "Gertrude Stein and Picasso: The Language of Surfaces." *American Literature* 45 (1973): 228–37.

Fodor, Jerry A., and Katz, Jerrold J., eds. *The Structure of Language: Readings in the Philosophy of Language.* Englewood Cliffs, New Jersey: Prentice-Hall, 1964.

Foley, Betty M. "The Ubicubist Joyce." *Ball State University Forum* 17 (Autumn 1976): 41–45.

Ford, Ford Madox. *Thus to Revisit: Some Reminiscences of Ford Madox Hueffer.* London: Chapman & Hall, 1921.

Forster, E.M. *Aspects of the Novel.* New York: Harcourt, Brace & Co., 1927.

Foucault, Michel. *The Archaeology of Knowledge and the Discourse on Language.* Translated by A.M. Sheridan Smith. New York: Pantheon Books, 1972.

———. "What Is an Author?". In Josué V. Harari, ed., *Textual Strategies: Perspectives in Post-Structuralist Criticism.* Ithaca: Cornell University Press, 1979.

Frank, Joseph. "Spatial Form in Modern Literature." *Sewanee Review* 53 (1945): 220–40.

Fry, Edward F., ed. *Cubism.* London: Thames & Hudson, 1966.

Fry, Roger. "M. Larionov and the Russian Ballet." *Burlington Magazine* 34 (1919): 112–18.

Frye, Northrop. *The Critical Path: An Essay on the Social Context of Literary Criticism.* Bloomington: Indiana University Press, 1973.

Gaither, Mary. "Literature and the Arts." In N.P. Stalknecht and Horst Freuz, eds., *Comparative Literature: Method and Perspective,* pp. 153–70. Carbondale: Southern Illinois University Press, 1961.

Gass, William. "Gertrude Stein: Her Escape from Protective Language." *Accent* 18 (Autumn 1958): 233–44.

Gibian, George, and H.W. Tjalsma, eds. *Russian Modernism: Culture and the Avant-Garde, 1900–1930.* Ithaca: Cornell University Press, 1976.

Giovanni, G. "Method in the Study of Literature in Its Relation to the Other Fine Arts." *Journal of Aesthetics and Art Criticism* 8 (March 1950): 185–95.

Golding, John. *Cubism: A History and Analysis, 1907–1914.* 2nd ed. New York: Harper & Row, 1968.

Goldwater, Robert, and Treves, Marco, eds. *Artists on Art, From the XIV to the XX Century.* New York: Pantheon Books, 1945.

Gorman, Herbert. *James Joyce.* New York: Farrar & Rinehart, 1939.

Gray, Camilla. *The Russian Experiment in Art, 1863-1922.* London: Thames and Hudson, 1962.

Gray, Christopher. *Cubist Aesthetic Theories.* Baltimore: Johns Hopkins Press, 1953.

Green, Christopher. *Léger and the Avant-Garde.* New Haven: Yale University Press, 1976.

Greenberg, Clement. *Art and Culture: Critical Essays.* Boston: Beacon Press, 1969.

Guiraud, Pierre. *Semiology.* London and Boston: Routledge and Kegan Paul, 1975.

Habasque, Guy. *Cubism: Biographical and Critical Study.* Translated by Stuart Gilbert. Geneva: Skira, 1959.

Hatzfeld, Helmut A. *Literature through Art.* New York: Oxford University Press, 1952.

Hauser, Arnold. *The Social History of Art.* Translated by Stanley Godman. New York: Vintage, 1958.

Henderson, Linda. "The Merging of Time and Space: 'The Fourth Dimension' in Russia from Ouspensky to Malevich." *The Structurist* 15/16 (1975/76): 87-108.

_____. "New Facets of Cubism: The Fourth Dimension and Non-Euclidean Geometry." *Art Quarterly* 34 (1971): 410-33.

Herbert, Robert L., ed. *Modern Artists on Art.* Englewood Cliffs, New Jersey: Prentice-Hall, 1964.

Higgins, Ian, ed. *Literature and the Plastic Arts 1880-1930: Seven Essays.* New York: Barnes & Noble, 1973.

Hoffman, Michael J. *The Development of Abstractionism in the Writings of Gertrude Stein.* Philadelphia: University of Pennsylvania Press, 1965.

Hopkins, Viola. "Visual Art Devices and Parallels in the Fiction of Henry James." *PMLA* 76 (1961): 561-74.

Howe, Irving, comp. *The Idea of the Modern in Literature and the Arts.* New York: Horizon Press, 1968.

Huddleston, Eugene L., and Noverr, Douglas A. *The Relationship of Painting and Literature: A Guide to Information Sources.* American Studies Information Guide Series, v. 4. Detroit: Gale Research, 1978.

Hulme, T.E. Quoted in "A Neglected Phase of British Art." *Apollo* 97 (March 1970): 174-85.

_____. *Speculations: Essays on Humanism and the Philosophy of Art.* Edited by Herbert Read. London: K. Paul, Trench, Trubner, 1924.

Hunt, John Dixon, ed. *Encounters: Essays on Literature and the Visual Arts.* London: Studio Vista, 1971.

Ingarden, Roman. *The Literary Work of Art: An Investigation on the Borderlines of Ontology, Logic, and Theory of Literature.* Translated by George G. Grabowicz. Evanston: Northwestern University Press, 1973.

Jakobson, Roman. "Modern Russian Poetry: Velimir Khlebnikov." Translated in Edward J. Brown. *Major Soviet Writers: Essays in Criticism,* pp. 58-82. London: Oxford University Press, 1973.

_____. "On the Verbal Art of William Blake and Other Poet-Painters." *Linguistic Inquiry* 1 (1970): 3-23.

_____. "Poetry of Grammar and Grammar of Poetry." *Lingua* 21 (1968): 597-609.

_____. *Questions de poétique.* Paris: Editions du Seuil, 1973.

_____. *Studies on Child Language and Aphasia.* The Hague: Mouton, 1971.

_____. "Two Aspects of Language and Two Types of Linguistic Disturbances." In Roman Jakobson and Morris Halle, *Fundamentals of Language.* The Hague: Mouton, 1956.

Jameson, Fredric. *Fables of Aggression: Wyndham Lewis, The Modernist as Fascist.* Berkeley: University of California Press, 1979.

————. *The Prison House of Language: A Critical Account of Structuralism and Russian Formalism.* Princeton: Princeton University Press, 1972.

————. "Wyndham Lewis as Futurist." *The Hudson Review* 26 (Summer 1973): 295–329.

Jarry, Alfred. *Selected Works.* Edited by Roger Shattuck and Simon Watson Taylor. London: Cape, 1965.

Joyce, James. *A Portrait of the Artist as a Young Man.* New York: Viking, 1964.

————. *Selected Letters.* Edited by Richard Ellmann. New York: Viking Press, 1957.

————. *Stephen Hero, A Part of the First Draft of "A Portrait of the Artist as a Young Man."* Edited by Theodore Spencer. New York: New Directions, 1944.

————. *Ulysses.* New York: Modern Library, 1946; Random House, 1961.

Judkins, Winthrop. "Toward a Reinterpretation of Cubism." *Art Bulletin* 30 (1948): 270–78.

Kahnweiler, Daniel Henry. *My Galleries and Painters.* Translated by Helen Weaver. New York: Viking Press, 1971.

————. *The Rise of Cubism.* Translated by Henry Aronson. New York: Wittenborn, Schultz, 1949.

Kamber, Gerald. *Max Jacob and the Poetics of Cubism.* Baltimore: Johns Hopkins Press, 1971.

Kandinsky, Wassily. *Concerning the Spiritual in Art, and Painting in Particular.* 1912. Translated by M.T.H. Sadleir with retranslation by Francis Golffing, Michael Harrison and Ferdinand Ostertag. Reprinted in *The Documents of Modern Art.* New York: Wittenborn, Schultz, 1947.

Karginov, German. *Rodchenko.* London: Thames & Hudson, 1979.

Kenner, Hugh. *The Pound Era.* Berkeley: University of California Press, 1971.

————. *Wyndham Lewis: The Makers of Modern Literature.* London: Methuen, 1954.

Kermode, Frank. *The Sense of an Ending.* New York: Oxford University Press, 1967.

Khlebnikov, Victor. *A Teacher and Pupil.* 1912. Cited by Vladimir Markov, *Russian Futurism—A History,* p. 40. London: MacGibbon & Kee, 1969.

"K.O.R.A.A." *transition* 3 (June 1927): 173–77.

Kristeva, Julia. *About Chinese Women.* Translated by Anita Barrows. London: Marion Boyars, 1977.

————. *Desire in Language: A Semiotic Approach to Literature and Art.* Edited by Leon S. Roudiez. Translated by Thomas Gora, Alice Jardine and Leon S. Roudiez. New York: Columbia University Press, 1980.

————. *Recherches pour une sémanalyse.* Paris: Editions du Seuil, 1969.

————. *Revolution in Poetic Language.* Translated by Margaret Waller with an Introduction by Leon S. Roudiez. New York: Columbia University Press, 1984.

————. "The Ruin of a Poetics." *20th Century Studies* 7/8 (December 1972): 102–21.

————. "The Subject in Signifying Practice." *Semiotext(e)* 1 (1974/75).

Kruchenykh, Aleksei. *Troe* [*The Three*]. Moscow: Zhuravl, 1913. Translated in Susan P. Compton, *The World Backwards: Russian Futurist Books 1912–1916,* p. 56. London: British Library, 1978.

Lacan, Jacques. *Ecrits.* Paris: Editions du Seuil, 1966. Translated by Alan Sheridan. New York, W.W. Norton, 1977.

————. *The Language of the Self: The Function of Language in Psychoanalysis.* Translated by Anthony Wilden. Baltimore: Johns Hopkins Press, 1968.

Lanthier, Philip J. "Vision and Satire in the Art and Fiction of Wyndham Lewis." Ph.D. dissertation, University of Toronto, 1972.

Laporte, Paul M. "Cubism and Science." *Journal of Aesthetics* 7 (1948): 244–66.

————. "The Space-Time Concept in the Work of Picasso." *Magazine of Art* 40 (1947): 26–29.

Larionov, Mikhail. "Rayonist Manifesto." Moscow, 1913. Quoted in Camilla Gray, *The Russian Experiment in Art, 1863–1922,* p. 138. London: Thames & Hudson, 1962.

Lemaître, Georges. *From Cubism to Surrealism in French Literature.* New York: Ungar, 1967.

Lessing, Gotthold Ephraim. *Laocoön: An Essay on the Limits of Painting and Poetry.* Translated by Edward Allen McCormick. Indianapolis: Bobbs-Merrill, 1962.

_____. *Selected Prose Works of G.E. Lessing.* Edited by Edward Bell. Translated by E.C. Beasley and Helen Zimmern. London: G. Bell, 1913.

Levin, David Michael. "The Novelhood of the Novel: The Limits of Representation and the Modernist Discovery of Presence." *Chicago Review* 28 (Spring 1977): 87–108.

Lewis, Wyndham. *Blasting and Bombardiering.* London: Eyre and Spottiswoode, 1937.

_____. *The Caliph's Design: Architects! Where Is Your Vortex?* London: Egoist, 1919.

_____. *The Demon of Progress in the Arts.* London: Methuen, 1954.

_____. "Enemy of the Stars." *Blast* 1 (1914): 51–86.

_____. *Enemy of the Stars.* London: Harmsworth, 1932.

_____. *The Letters of Wyndham Lewis.* Edited by W.K. Rose. London: Methuen, 1963.

_____. *One-Way Song.* London: Methuen, 1960.

_____. "A Review of Contemporary Art." *Blast* 2 (July 1915): 38–47.

_____. *Rude Assignment, A Narrative of My Career Up-to-Date.* London: Hutchinson, 1950.

_____. "The Russian Ballet, The Most Perfect Expression of the High Bohemia." *The Enemy: A Review of Art and Literature* 1 (1927–29). Reprint ed., New York: Kraus Reprint, 1967: 54–57.

_____. *Time and Western Man.* London: Chatto and Windus, 1927.

_____, ed. *The Tyro, A Review of Art and Literature.* No. 1–2. London: Egoist Press, 1921–22. Reprint ed., London: Frank Cass, 1970.

_____. "Vortices and Notes." *Blast* 1 (1914): 129–49.

_____. "The Vorticists." *Vogue* (September 1956): 216.

_____. *Wyndham Lewis on Art: Collected Writings 1913–1956.* Edited by Walter Michel and C.J. Fox. New York: Funk & Wagnalls, 1969.

Lieven, Peter. *The Birth of Ballets-Russes.* Translated by L. Zarine. London: Allen & Unwin, 1956.

Lissitzky-Küppers, Sophie, ed. *El Lissitzky: Life, Letters, Texts.* London, 1980.

Livshits, Benedikt. "Liberation of the Word." *The Crooked Moon.* Moscow: Oysen, 1914. Quoted in Susan P. Compton, "Malevich's Suprematism—The Higher Intuition." *Burlington Magazine* 118 (August 1976): 577–85.

_____. *Polutoraglazyi Strelets.* Leningrad, 1933. Cited in Susan P. Compton, *The World Backwards: Russian Futurist Books 1912–1916*, p. 55. London: British Library, 1978.

Lodder, Christina, *Russian Constructivism.* New Haven and London: Yale University Press, 1983.

Loss, Archie K. "Interior and Exterior Imagery in the Earlier Work of Joyce and Symbolist Art." *Journal of Modern Literature* 8 (1980): 99–117.

Lukács, Georg. *The Meaning of Contemporary Realism.* London: Merlin Press, 1963.

Lyotard, Jean-François. *The Post-Modern Condition: A Report on Knowledge.* Translated by Geoff Bennington and Brian Massumi. Minneapolis: University of Minnesota Press, 1984.

McMillan, Samuel H. "Gertrude Stein, the Cubists and the Futurists." Ph.D. dissertation, University of Texas, 1964.

Malevich, Kazimir. *Essays on Art 1915–1933.* Edited by Troels Andersen. Translated by Xenia Glowacki-Prus and Arnold McMillin. London: Rapp & Whiting, 1969.

_____. *The Non-Objective World.* Translated by Howard Dearstyne. Chicago: P. Theobald, 1959.

Mallarmé, Stéphane. Preface; *Un Coup de dés jamais n'abolira le hasard.* Translated by Daisy Ablan. *Folder* 4 (1956), Tiber Press.

Marinetti, Filippo Tommaso. *Marinetti: Selected Writings.* Edited by R.W. Flint and Arthur A. Coppotelli. New York: Farrar, Straus and Giroux, 1972.

Markov, Vladimir. *Russian Futurism—A History.* London: MacGibbon & Kee, 1969.

Marks, Elaine, and de Courtivron, Isabelle. *New French Feminism: An Anthology.* New York: Schocken Books, 1981.

Martin, Marianne. "Futurism, Unanimism and Apollinaire." *Art Journal* 28/29 (1969): 258-63.

_____. *Futurist Art and Theory.* Oxford: Clarendon, 1968.

Matyushin, M. "Futurizm v peterburge." *Futuristy: Pervyi jhurnal russkikh futuristov* 1/2 (1914). Cited in Charlotte Douglas, "Birth of a 'Royal Infant': Malevich and *Victory over the Sun,"* 47. *Art in America* 62 (March/April 1974): 45-63.

Mayakofsky, Vladimir. "Vladimir Mayakofsky, A Tragedy." *TDR/ The Drama Review* 15 (Fall 1971): 80-91.

"Meeting ob iskusstve." *Iskusstvo Kommuni* 1 (December 7, 1918). Cited by Camilla Gray, *The Russian Experiment in Art, 1863-1922*, p. 219. London: Thames & Hudson, 1962.

Mellow, James R. "Gertrude Stein among the Dadaists." *Arts Magazine* (May 1977): 124-27.

Merleau-Ponty, Maurice. "Cézanne's Doubt." In *Sense and Non-Sense.* Translated by Hubert L. Dreyfus and Patricia Allen Dreyfus. Evanston: Northwestern University Press, 1964.

Merriman, James D. "The Parallel of the Arts: Some Misgivings and a Faint Affirmation." *The Journal of Aesthetics and Art Criticism* 31 (Winter 1972): 153-64; (Spring 1973): 309-21.

Milner, John. *Vladimir Tatlin and the Russian Avant-Garde.* New Haven and London: Yale University Press, 1985.

Mitchell, Juillet. *Psychoanalysis and Feminism.* Harmondsworth: Allen Lane, 1975.

Moi, Toril. *Sexual/Textual Politics: Feminist Literary Theory.* London and New York: Methuen, 1985.

Morse, J. Mitchell, "Karl Gutzkow and the Novel of Simultaneity." *James Joyce Quarterly* 2 (1964): 13-17.

Motherwell, Robert, ed. *The Dada Painters and Poets: An Anthology.* New York: Wittenborn, Schultz, 1951.

Mukařovský, Jan. "Dialectic Contradictions in Modern Art." In *Structure, Sign, and Function: Selected Essays.* New Haven: Yale University Press, 1978.

_____. "Standard Language and Poetic Language." In Paul L. Garvin, ed., *A Prague School Reader on Esthetics, Literary Structure and Style.* Washington: Georgetown University Press, 1964.

_____. *The Word and Verbal Art: Selected Essays by Jan Mukařovský.* Edited and translated by John Burbank and Peter Steiner. New Haven: Yale University Press, 1977.

Munro, Thomas. *The Arts and Their Interrelations.* Cleveland: Case Western Reserve Press, 1969.

"A Neglected Phase of British Art." Editorial. *Apollo* (March 1917), 182.

Neumann, Alfred R., Erdman, David B., et al. *Literature and the Other Arts: A Selected Bibliography, 1952-1958.* New York: New York Public Library, 1959. Supplements published as *A Bibliography on the Relations of Literature and the Other Arts*, collected under the auspices of the M.L.A. Discusssion Group, 1965.

Nevinson, Christopher. Interview in *New York Times* (May 1919). Cited by Richard Cork, *Vorticism and Abstract Art in the First Machine Age*, v. 2, p. 512. Berkeley: University of California Press, 1976.

_____. Interview in *The Studio* (December 1919). Cited by Richard Cork, *Vorticism and Abstract Art in the First Machine Age*, vol. 2, p. 512. Berkeley: University of California Press, 1976.

Nietzsche, Friedrich. *Der Wille zur Macht: Versuch einer Umwerthung aller Werthe.* Leipzig: Naumann, 1901. Cited by Christopher Middleton, *Bolshevism in Art and Other Expository Writings*, p. 285. Manchester: Carcanet New Press, 1978.

O'Connell, Daniel. *The Opposition Critics: The Antisymbolist Reaction in the Modern Period.* (The Hague/Paris: Mouton, 1974).

"The Omega Workshops Ltd." In *Catalogue of the Ideal Home Exhibition*. London: *Daily Mail*, 1913.

Ortega y Gasset, José. *The Dehumanization of Art, and Other Writings on Art and Culture*. Translated by Willard A. Trask. Garden City, New York: Doubleday, 1956.

Panofsky, Erwin. *Meaning in the Visual Arts*. Garden City, New York: Doubleday, 1955.

———. *Studies in Iconology*. New York: Harper & Row, 1962.

Pater, Walter. "The School of Giorgione." In *The Renaissance*, 1873. Reprint ed., pp. 126–44. New York: Modern Library, 1961.

Paz, Octavio. *Marcel Duchamp: Appearance Stripped Bare*. Translated by Rachel Phillips and Donald Gardner. New York: Viking, [1978].

Peirce, Charles Sanders. *Collected Papers*. 8 vols. Cambridge: Harvard University Press, 1931–58.

Penrose, Roland, and Golding, John, eds. *Picasso in Retrospect*. New York: Praeger, 1973.

Perloff, Marjorie. "Poetry as Word-System: The Art of Gertrude Stein." *The American Poetry Review* 8 (September/October 1979): 33–44.

Peterson, Dale E. "Nabokov's *Invitation*: Literature as Execution." *PMLA* 96 (October 1981): 824–36.

Poggioli, Renato. *The Poets of Russia 1890–1930*. Cambridge: Harvard University Press, 1960.

———. *The Spirit of the Letter: Essays in European Literature*. Cambridge: Harvard University Press, 1965.

———. *The Theory of the Avant Garde*. Translated by Gerald Fitzgerald. Cambridge: Harvard University Press, 1968.

Pound, Ezra. "Brancusi." 1921. In *Literary Essays of Ezra Pound*. Edited by T.S. Eliot, pp. 441–45. London: Faber and Faber, 1954.

———. *The Cantos of Ezra Pound*. New York: New Directions, 1934.

———. *Gaudier-Brzeska: A Memoir*. New York: New Directions, 1960.

———. *Hugh Selwyn Mauberley*. London: Ovid Press, 1920.

———. *The Letters of Ezra Pound*. Edited by D.D. Paige. London: Faber and Faber, 1951.

———. *Literary Essays of Ezra Pound*. Edited by T.S. Eliot. London: Faber and Faber, 1954.

———. *Make It New: Essays*. London: Faber and Faber, 1934.

———. "The New Sculpture." *The Egoist* 1 (February 16, 1914).

———. "Prologomena." *Poetry Review* 1 (February 1912): 72–76.

———. "Vortex." *Blast* 1 (1914): 153–55.

———. "Vorticism" (1). *Fortnightly Review* (September 1, 1914): 461–71.

Praz, Mario. *Mnemosyne: The Parallel between Literature and the Visual Arts*. Princeton: Princeton University Press, 1970.

"Proclamation." *transition* 16/17 (June 1929): 13.

Raymond, Marcel. *From Baudelaire to Surrealism*. London: Methuen, 1970.

Rexroth, Kenneth. *Birds in the Bush: Obvious Essays*. New York: New Directions, [1959].

Riddel, Joseph. "Decentering the Image: The Project of 'American' Poetics?" In Josué V. Harari, ed., *Textual Strategies: Perspectives in Post-Structuralist Criticism*, pp. 325–45. Ithaca: Cornell University Press, 1979.

Robbe-Grillet, Alain. *Snapshots, and Towards a New Novel*. Translated by Barbara Wright. London: Calder & Boyars, 1965.

Robbins, Daniel. "From Symbolism to Cubism: The Abbaye of Créteil." *Art Journal* 22/23 (1962–64): 111–16.

Rose, Margaret. *Marx's Lost Aesthetic: Karl Marx and the Visual Arts*. Cambridge: Cambridge University Press, 1984.

Rose, Marilyn Gaddis. "Gertrude Stein and the Cubist Narrative." *Modern Fiction Studies* 22 (1976/77): 543–55.

Rosenblum, Robert. *Cubism and Twentieth-Century Art.* New York: Abrams, 1966.

——. "Picasso and the Typography of Cubism." In Roland Penrose and John Golding, eds., *Picasso in Retrospect.* New York: Praeger, 1973.

Sapir, Edward. *Selected Writings in Language, Culture and Personality.* Edited by David G. Mandelbaum. Berkeley: University of California Press, 1949.

Saussure, Ferdinand de. *Course in General Linguistics.* Translated by Wade Baskin. Edited by Charles Bally and Albert Sechehaye. New York: McGraw-Hill, 1966.

Saxl, Fritz. *A Heritage of Images: A Selection of Lectures.* Harmondsworth, Middlesex: Penguin, 1970.

Schmitz, Neil. "Gertrude Stein as Post-Modernist: The Rhetoric of *Tender Buttons.*" *Journal of Modern Literature* 3 (1974): 1203–19.

——. "Portrait, Patriarchy, Mythos: The Revenge of Gertrude Stein." *Salmagundi* 40 (Winter 1978).

Scholes, Robert. *Structuralism in Literature: An Introduction.* New Haven: Yale University Press, 1974.

Shapiro, Meyer. "On Some Problems in the Semiotics of Visual Art: Field and Vehicle in Image-Signs." *Semiotica* 1 (1969).

Shattuck, Roger. *The Banquet Years: The Arts in France 1895–1918.* London: Faber and Faber, 1959.

Smitten, Jeffrey R., and Daghistany, Ann. *Spatial Form in Narrative.* Ithaca: Cornell University Press, 1981.

Sokel, Walter. *The Writer in Extremis.* Princeton: Princeton University Press, 1965.

Stein, Gertrude. *The Autobiography of Alice B. Toklas.* New York: Harcourt, Brace, [1933].

——. "Composition as Explanation." In *Selected Writings of Gertrude Stein.* Edited by Carl Van Vechten. New York: Random House, [1946].

——. *Everybody's Autobiography.* New York: Random House, 1937. Reprint ed., New York: Cooper Square, 1971.

——. *The Geographical History of America or The Relation of Human Nature to the Human Mind.* New York: Random House, 1936; Reprint ed., New York: Vintage Books, 1973.

——. *Geography and Plays.* New York: Haskell House, 1967.

——. *Gertrude Stein on Picasso.* Edited by Edward Burns. New York: Liveright, 1970.

——. "The Gradual Making of *The Making of Americans.*" In *Lectures in America*, pp. 135–61. New York: Random House, 1935.

——. *How to Write.* Barton, Vermont: Something Else Press, 1973.

——. *How Writing Is Written: Volume II of the Previously Uncollected Writings of Gertrude Stein.* Edited by Robert Bartlett Haas. Los Angeles: Black Sparrow Press, 1974

——. "Lecture 2." In *Narration: Four Lectures*, pp. 16–29. Chicago: University of Chicago Press, 1935.

——. *Lectures in America.* New York: Random House, 1935.

——. *The Making of Americans, Being a History of a Family's Progress.* Paris: Contact, 1925; Condensed ed. New York: Harcourt, Brace, 1934.

——. "Mildred Aldrich Saturday." In *Portraits and Prayers*, pp. 111–23. New York: Random House, (1934).

——. *Narration: Four Lectures.* Chicago: University of Chicago Press, 1935.

——. *A Novel of Thank You.* New Haven: Yale University Press, 1958.

——. "Picasso." In *Selected Writings of Gertrude Stein.* Edited by Carl Van Vechten. New York: Random House, [1946].

——. *Picasso.* 1912; Reprint ed., London: Batsford, 1939.

——. "Pictures." In *Lectures in America*, pp. 59–90. New York: Random House, 1935.

——. "Poetry and Grammar." In *Lectures in America*, pp. 209–46. New York: Random House, 1935.

———. "Portraits and Repetition." In *Lectures in America*, pp. 165–206. New York: Random House, 1935.

———. *A Primer for the Gradual Understanding of Gertrude Stein*. Edited by Robert Bartlett Haas. Los Angeles: Black Sparrow Press, 1971.

———. *Selected Writings of Gertrude Stein*. Edited by Carl Van Vechten. New York: Random House, [1946].

———. *Tender Buttons: Objects, Food, Rooms*. New York: C. Marie, 1914.

———. *Three Lives: Stories of the Good Anna, Melanctha, and the Gentle Lena*. New York: Random House, 1909.

———. "A Transatlantic Interview 1946." In *A Primer for the Gradual Understanding of Gertrude Stein*. Edited by Robert Bartlett Haas, pp. 11–35. Los Angeles: Black Sparrow Press, 1971.

———. *Writings and Lectures 1911–1945*. Edited by Patricia Meyerowitz. London: Owen, (1967).

Stein, Leo. *Appreciation: Painting, Poetry and Prose*. New York: Crown, 1947.

———. *Journey into the Self: Being the Letters, Papers, and Journals of Leo Stein*. Edited by Edmund Fuller. New York: Crown, 1950.

Steinberg, Leo. "The Philosophical Brothel." *Art News* 71 (1972): 21–25.

Steiner, Wendy. *The Colors of Rhetoric: Problems in the Relation between Modern Literature and Painting*. Chicago: University of Chicago Press, 1982.

———. *Exact Resemblance to Exact Resemblance: The Literary Portraiture of Gertrude Stein*. New Haven: Yale University Press, 1978.

Sypher, Wylie. *Rococo to Cubism in Art and Literature*. New York: Random House, 1960.

Tashjian, Dickran. *Skyscraper Primitives: Dada and the American Avant-Garde, 1910–1925*. Middleton, Conn.: Wesleyan University Press, 1975.

Tatlin, V.E. *Ezhednevnii Bulletin S'ezda* 13 (1921): 11. Cited by Camilla Gray, *The Russian Experiment in Art, 1863–1922*, p. 219. London: Thames & Hudson, 1962.

Taylor, Joshua C. *Futurism*. New York: Museum of Modern Art, 1961.

Thomson, Virgil. Preface and notes to Gertrude Stein, *Bee Time Vine, and Other Pieces, 1913–1927*. New Haven: Yale University Press, 1953.

———. *Virgil Thomson*. New York: Knopf, 1967.

Todorov, Tzvetan. *Introduction to Poetics*. Translated by Richard Howard. Minneapolis: University of Minnesota Press, 1981.

291. Nos. 1–12 (March 1915–February 1916). New York, Arno Press, 1972.

Tomaskevsky, Kolia. "Vladimir Mayakovsky." *Teatr* 4 (1938). Translated by Ewa Bartos and Victoria Nes Kirby in *TDR/The Drama Review* 15 (Fall 1971): 99–101.

Tzara, Tristan. *Seven Dada Manifestos and Lampisteries*. Translated by Barbara Wright. London: Calder, 1977.

Uspensky, Boris. *The Semiotics of the Russian Icon*. Edited by Stephen Rudy. Translated by P.A. Reed. 1922; Reprint ed., Lisse: P. de Ridder Press, 1976.

Vengerova, Zinaida. "Angliiskie futuristy." *Strelets* 1 (1915): 93–94. Unpublished translation by John Barnstead.

Victory over the Sun. Translated by Ewa Bartos and Victoria Nes Kirby. *TDR/The Drama Review* 15 (Fall 1971): 92–123.

Vygotsky, Lev Seenovich. *Thought and Language*. Edited and translated by Eugenia Hanfmann and Gertrude Vakar. Cambridge: M.I.T. Press, 1962.

Wadsworth, Edward. Review of *Concerning the Spiritual in Art, and Painting in Particular*, by Wassily Kandinsky. *Blast* 1 (1914): 119–28.

Waldrop, Keith. "Gertrude Stein's Tears." *Novel* (Spring 1979): 236–43.

Wasserstrom, William. "The Sursymamericubealism of Gertrude Stein." *Twentieth Century Literature* 21 (1975): 90–106.

Wees, William C. *Vorticism and the English Avant-Garde.* Toronto: University of Toronto Press, 1972.

Whorf, Benjamin L. *Language, Thought and Reality.* Edited by John B. Carroll. Cambridge: M.I.T. Press, 1956.

Williams, William Carlos. "A 1 Pound Stein." In *Selected Essays of William Carlos Williams.* New York: New Directions, 1954.

––––––. *Autobiography.* New York: New Directions, 1951.

Wilson, Edmund. *Axel's Castle: A Study in the Imaginative Literature of 1820 to 1930.* New York: Scribner, 1931.

Wittgenstein, Ludwig. *Tractatus Logico-Philosophicus.* Cited by David Michael Levin. "The Novelhood of the Novel: The Limits of Representation and the Modernist Discovery of Presence," pp. 90–91. *Chicago Review* 28 (Spring 1977): 87–108.

Worringer, Wilhelm. *Abstraction and Empathy: A Contribution to the Psychology of Style, 1908.* Translated by Michael Bullock. New York: International Universities Press, [1967].

Zhadova, Larissa A. *Malevich: Suprematism and Revolution in Russian Art 1910–1930.* Translated by Alexander Lieven. London: Thames & Hudson, 1982.

Index

Index and bibliography prepared by Margaret MacKay